Discover
THE TRUE WONDER WOMAN IN YOU

Find and Release
Your God-Given Powers

By
EVELYN MORALES

Copyright © 2016 by Evelyn Morales

Discover The True Wonder Woman In You
Find and Release Your God-Given Powers
by Evelyn Morales

Printed in the United States of America.

ISBN 9781498470308

All rights reserved solely by the author. The author guarantees all contents are original and do not infringe upon the legal rights of any other person or work. No part of this book may be reproduced in any form without the permission of the author. The views expressed in this book are not necessarily those of the publisher.

Scripture quotations taken from the New International Version (NIV). Copyright © 1973, 1978, 1984, 2011 by International Bible Society. Used by permission. All rights reserved.

Scripture quotations taken from the New Living Translation (NLT). Copyright © 1996, 2004, 2007 by Tyndale House Foundation. Used by permission. All rights reserved.

Scripture quotations taken from the English Standard Version (ESV). Copyright © 2001 by Crossway, a publishing ministry of Good News Publishers. Used by permission. All rights reserved.

Scripture quotations taken from the New American Standard Bible (NASB). Copyright © 1960, 1962, 1963, 1968, 1971, 1972, 1973, 1975, 1977, 1995 by The Lockman Foundation. Used by permission. All rights reserved.

Scripture quotations taken from the King James Version (KJV) – *public domain*

Scripture quotations taken from the Amplified Bible (AMP). Copyright © 1954, 1958, 1962, 1964, 1965, 1987 by The Lockman Foundation. Used by permission. All rights reserved.

Author's Note: This book contains true stories of women's lives, and all names herein have been changed to protect their identities.

Contact Evie:
eviewwb@gmail.com
Facebook: Evie Morales

www.xulonpress.com

This book is dedicated

To my adoring husband, Dr. Maynor Morales (my Superman). Thank you for supporting me throughout this journey. Your love, wisdom, and godly character have shaped my life these past thirty years for the better. Thank you also for helping me with revising the whole manuscript. I appreciate your wise counsel and I love you forever. I would also like to dedicate this book to my wonderful daughters, Krystal and Tiffany. You are true wonder women in the making amidst this twenty-first century, postmodern world. Thank you for your love, support and patience. I am so proud of having such great, loving daughters.

Table of Contents

Acknowledgments ix
Foreword xiii
Introduction xvii

1   The Rise and Fall of the First True
    Wonder Woman 25

2   Elevating the True Wonder Woman to His Glory 57

3   Traits of a True Wonder Woman: Part 1 71
    Spiritual Warrior: Part 2 101

4   Beating the Do it All Syndrome 113

5   Conquering the Traumas of Sexual Abuse 137

6   Can Wonder Woman Be Hormonal and Still
    Save the Day? 167

7   God's True Wonder Woman's Fashion 189

8   Celebrate the True Wonder Woman in You 213

    Notes 227

    About the Author 235

Acknowledgments

A special thanks to…

To my **Heavenly Father, Jesus Christ**, and **the Holy Spirit**, who empowers me daily with strength and wisdom. Thank you for your unconditional love and for guiding my path as I walk on this journey, continually discovering the true wonder woman in me. I want to thank my dad, **Noel Guerra**, who exemplifies a life filled with joy, faith, and hope. *Thank you Dad for your prayers and for teaching me how to trust God through it all.* I would also like to acknowledge two genuine Godly women who went to be with the Lord. They left a legacy of faithfulness and perseverance in His service. They were my mother, **Carmen Guerra,** who was a prayer warrior and taught me that battles are fought on our knees; also, my mother-in-law, **Silveria Morales**, a woman of faith, who countless times counseled me on how to endure with resilience the hardships of ministry. They were warriors in His kingdom that embodied a Christ-like character and made a difference in me while I was growing up. They were God's true wonder women who fought fiercely the vicissitudes of their lifetime, and lived victoriously because of their trust in the Lord.

Rev. Rosy Barrios, this book would not have existed if it wasn't for the fact that you gave me an opportunity to be part of your staff at the Northern Pacific Latin American District Women's Ministry. This book was inspired by the seminar I gave called "Discover the Wonder Woman in You," at Washington State back in 2009 when we traveled together. Thank you for believing in me and allowing my crazy creativity come to life. It was an honor to work with you. You are an amazing woman of God!

I would also like to thank my friends and the women I have encountered in my ministerial journey, who are mentioned in this book. Thank you for allowing me to share your experiences with others. Furthermore, I would like to recognize the following ladies. My life has been enriched by knowing each of you. You have impacted me in so many different ways positively with your devout and holy lives. You are truly wonder women in God's book and in mines. **Rev. Esther Cuevas**, thank you for your great friendship. Your words of encouragement, prayers, and generosity ministered to me when the going got tough. I miss those long hours chatting at your office in New Dawn Worship Center. **Leticia Sandoval**, truly you are a rare and beautiful jewel, a model of Christ-like character for women to follow. **Rev. Jacqueline Ramos, Rev. Martha Sanchez, Isabel Garcia, Kattya Kancylarysta, Luz Maria Aguirre, Edith Maltez, Lisa Bacon, Auntie Brunilda Rodriguez,** and my cousin **Marilyn Guettouche**, your prayers, support and genuine

Acknowledgments

love have definitely made a mark in my heart. I Love you immensely.

Irene Cruz, and **Kaylee Parsons,** thank you so much for taking time out of your busy schedule to revise the first part of my manuscript. I appreciate your support toward this project. Special thanks to my editor **Sally Casey.** I was truly blessed to have found you. You did a great job in perfecting my work. I do not know what I would have done without you. God bless you. **Rev. Alicia Martinez** thanks for wonderfully creating the pictures for this book. You are so talented! **Mabel Guerra** thanks for being there for the family in the hard times. You've been a great sister-in-law. Please know that you are loved.

Last but not least, I would also like to acknowledge my other two sisters-in-law and also my brothers-in-law's wives. In my view, you are all astounding, godly wonder women with unique traits. You have blessed my life in many different ways. **Rev. Olga Marina Morales, Rev. Reyna Guzman, Rev. Sara Jane Morales, Rev. Carlota Morales, Rev. Maryelen Morales, and Esther Morales**; Your devotion to God's service is worthy to be recognized and modeled by others.

Foreword

It has always been an honor and a joy to serve the Lord as Senior Pastor of La Nueva Jerusalen, but God knew that my heart wanted more than to pastor a church. He knew that my heart also yearned to reach people—especially broken women—who live outside the four walls of the church. It was the year 2008 when the Lord placed a calling upon my heart to work as the woman's director for the Northern Pacific Latin American District of Assemblies of God (NPLAD). This position required training women in leadership, organizing women's conventions and events, and ministering to hundreds of women. I have to say that taking up this position was a leap of faith. I knew that the Lord had called me to do this work, but I had no clue how I would do it, nor who would help me. As I prayed to the Lord for direction and help, He led me to a group of talented, skillful and spiritual women that became part of my team. These women assisted me in leadership training and all that pertained to women's ministry. Amongst these marvelous women, I was truly blessed to have Evelyn (Evie) Morales be part of my team.

The first time I saw Evie was at a NPLAD Minister's Convention. She was not only a pastor's wife; she also had a singing ministry, and often was asked to sing at our conventions. I met her through a friend and instantly my spirit connected with hers. I learned that she shared my passion to minister to the needs of women. It was a great adventure to work with my team, especially with Evie.

Those of us who know her can attest to her quick wit. She has a great sense of humor and she is very real! We never had a dull moment around her. On one occasion, after spending a long day ministering at a conference in the state of Washington, our team decided to go out and get some dinner. While we were waiting for our dinner to be served, Evie pulled out a long pill container. I asked her, "What are those?" She replied, "They are my vitamins. I always bring them with me when I travel. These vitamins are good for you: they make your body and mind stronger." I noticed that she looked troubled and asked, "Evie, what are you looking for?" With a puzzled look on her face, she said, "Oh, I'm looking for my brain enhancement vitamins, and I can't seem to remember which one of these pills they are!" Everyone at the table bursted with laughter! We laughed so much that we forgot that we were tired. This is just one example of the many ways that Evie brought so much joy to our team.

Not only does Evie have a great sense of humor, she is also spontaneous, talented, dynamic, and knowledgeable in God's Word. She is a woman of integrity that embodies a Christ-like character. In the three years that I worked with her, she demonstrated the spirit of a warrior who was not afraid of tackling challenges head on or doing things outside of the box. When we started our women's ministry, we confronted issues that no one dared to speak about in our district. Evie was the first one to break ground in addressing topics such as how to receive inner healing from sexual and domestic abuse, and what God's Word tells Christian women about how to deal with hormonal behavior, and much more. Evie brought every subject to the table successfully: with love and wisdom, and with God's anointing. Her work has been a blessing to my life and to our women's ministry.

With this book, Evie has crafted an excellent tool for women who are seeking to be empowered by the knowledge of God's Word. Every chapter teaches us how to depend on God's strength in order to successfully deal with life's personal battles. It explains how to overcome the spiritual ones as well. Evie covers a variety of subjects that are relevant to the needs of the women of today. She speaks with God's authority in a gentle and loving way that can minister to the soul of a woman. *Discovering the True Wonder Woman in You* will be a blessing for women, both as private reading material and as part of woman's gatherings at church. This book serves as a guide to help women find their true identity and inner strength in Christ. As you read it, you will be motivated to discover the true wonder woman in you.

Rev. Rosy Barrios

Visalia, California

March 8, 2016

Reverend Rosy Barrios is the Director of Women's Ministry of the Northern Pacific Latin American District of Assemblies of God, where she has served for over eight years and is also the Senior Pastor of La Nueva Jerusalen church in Visalia, California.

Introduction

Wonder Woman was a superheroine created by William Moulton Marston in the early 1940s, and she has graced the pages of DC Comics' publications almost continually since then. As a child, I used to collect comic books featuring many different heroes, but Wonder Woman was my favorite one. Years later, around the mid-70s, she was brought to life in the *Wonder Woman* television series starring Linda Carter. I watched her show religiously. Women and girls all over the world wanted to be like her, and I was one of them.

During my sixth grade year, when attending gym class, my classmates and I competed in relay races. I vividly remember the kids cheering for me energetically: "Go Wonder Woman! You can do it—you can win the race!" You might be wondering why on earth my classmates called me "Wonder Woman." It was not because I was as fast and furious as she was. I was a skimpy, skinny thing that barely had enough strength to make it to the finish line. They called me that name because every time I ran a race, I would wear an outfit similar to that which

Wonder Woman wore: including a cape, her famous lasso, bracelets, and a crown embedded with a star that looked like the one she wore on her forehead. Yes, I must admit that it felt like I was going to a costume party every time I had gym class. Although I was teased, it didn't matter to me because I profoundly admired this woman for what she represented, and I dreamt of being just like her.

To this day, I still ask myself, "Why do women admire this fictional comic book character so much?" Is it because of her heroic demeanor? She is determined, she is sensitive to the needs of others, and she strives to serve and protect people. Is it because of her beauty and special abilities? She can fly (as of the 1980s) and has great strength. She can deflect flying bullets with her magic bracelets, and let's not forget that she's gorgeous. We often find ourselves drawn to such heroic characters that have the strength to conquer anything and have the traits that we feel we lack. However, we must remember that we live in the real world, we confront real problems, and we all have a spiritual enemy. As much as we admire this fictional character, realistically speaking, we cannot go around and function in our everyday lives dressed up in a Wonder Woman costume, thinking that we can turn ourselves into that exact character and be able to overcome life's vicissitudes with our own strength.

As human beings, we yearn for the strength and power to overcome life's battles, but time and again we find ourselves struggling just to make it to the end of each and every day. Throughout my thirty years in ministry as an evangelist, a conference speaker, and an associate pastor, I have witnessed numerous women who lived emotionally and spiritually broken lives with a shattered faith in their true identity in

Introduction

Christ. The trials of life left many feeling helpless and beaten; therefore, they were no longer able to recognize their God-given powers.

Most of these women often spent their time giving themselves wholeheartedly to others: caring for young ones, elderly parents, ministries, careers, work, and so forth. They were admirable women, but somehow along the way, in the midst of their trials and busy lives, they neglected to make time to care for themselves and nurture their relationship with God. As a result, they were unable to successfully balance life and were left feeling frustrated and unaccomplished. Ultimately, they were hindered from reaching their full potential, unable to develop their hidden talents, and inhibited from experiencing inner growth. To illustrate, here are two stories: one about Roselyn and one about Jan (their real names have been changed).

Roselyn was a young housewife who was filled with wonderful goals for herself and for her family to serve God in ministry at her local church. She loved the Lord, her husband, and her children very much. This motivated her to be the best mother and wife that she could be. There came a time when financial hardships drove her back to the workforce. She worked long hours and spent less and less time with her husband and children. Weary work days, household chores, late-night cooking, and after-school care pickups made her irritable and exhausted. Her husband's lack of support in all these areas intensified her fatigue and frustration. Furthermore, their prayer life, romance, and communication began to decay, which led to the decline of her marriage.

Unfortunately, Roselyn did not know how to balance work and family. She also did not take time to care for herself and her spiritual life. Somewhere down the road, she disconnected herself from God. Feeling drained and vulnerable, she drifted farther away from the Lord and her marriage. The enemy waited for an opportunity to tempt her with another man whom she felt attracted to at her job. She began to pay a little more attention to his flirtatious looks and sweet words. One day he asked her out on a lunch date. At first, she thought to herself, "Well, an innocent lunch will do no harm." Little did she know that she was falling into the devil's trap. That lunch date led to many more dates and ended up turning into an adulterous affair. It tore her family apart and halted her goals to pursue her God-given ministry.

Jan, another vibrant young woman, had great potential to exercise her gifts at her local church. However, along with her gifts, she had a hurtful past that hindered her from pursuing God's plan for her life. She was molested as a child. This trauma ultimately left her with tremendously low self-esteem, which kept her from moving forward in her ministry and fulfilling heaven's purposes for her for a long time. However, one Sunday night, she found freedom in Jesus and submitted her hurt to God. She forgave her trespasser, and through the power of the Holy Spirit and the guidance of His Word, she became the special wonder woman that Christ destined her to be.

If you are a woman like Roselyn or Jan and are confronting similar (or different) difficulties or whose inner strength, dreams, and image have been crushed by Satan and by the adversities of life, allow me to encourage you through this book. In 2009, I was invited to speak at a women's conference in the state of Washington. I spoke on the subject, "Discover the Wonder Woman in You," which encouraged women to find their strength and power in Jesus in order to become that special superwoman. I used Wonder Woman as an introduction and example of the type of woman we each would like to be and can be through Christ. One night, as I was reflecting on the needs of the women that I had come across, my heart was touched with compassion. With a humble heart, I remembered the positive feedback that I received from women who attended that conference, which motivated me to write this book with the purpose of reaching out to women who are feeling powerless and have not yet discovered the true wonder woman in them.

How can we discover the true wonder woman that God designed us to be, and how can we overcome our trials, temptations, past traumas, and Satan, our spiritual enemy? It is important that we keenly strive to find, utilize, and release our God-given powers in order to overcome our shortcomings and live triumphantly. This book, *Discover the True Wonder Woman in You*, is not just another self-help book about discovering who you are or what you can achieve by your own natural human abilities; but rather, it is about discovering all that God wants you to be and all that you can achieve through His divine power. The purpose of this book is to bring a message of *hope* to all women and provide them with the necessary biblical tools of *empowerment* for victorious living. Victorious living cannot be attained until we fully believe, understand, and accept that: ***We were Wonderfully created by a Wonderful God to do Wonders in His name.*** There may be many wonder women in the world, but the *true* wonder woman is distinguished by the fact that she possesses a supernatural power solely given by the Holy Spirit, and God wants to equip you with this special power.

In this book, you will find the experiences of real women who have dealt with real problems and hard situations which you and I can relate to. These women include my friends, family, and those I have encountered throughout my years in ministry. I have used fictitious names in order to protect their true identities for the sake of their privacy. We will learn how most of them found strength in Christ to overcome their obstacles. The purpose of these stories is to illustrate that many other women have struggled with the same problems that we are facing. It is comforting to know that not only are we not alone, but also that as women, we need each other for encouragement.

I have a special message to all of the wonderful working moms, house wives, single moms, career women, single women, women in ministry, and all women of all walks of life who strive to find a balance in everything that they do: When you stay connected with God and remain dependent on Him, you will find refuge, inner strength, and power. He will endow you with wisdom to navigate through the rough seas that you will encounter in life. There is a true wonder woman in you, just waiting to be discovered. Can you see her?

Chapter One

To create a woman was always part of God's eternal plan. Although sin came through a woman, salvation also came through the womb of a woman.

The Rise and Fall of the First True Wonder Woman

Can there be such a thing as a perfect woman? Our modern culture has created an influential blueprint of the ideal woman. She must be a size 2 at all times, look like a model, have flawless skin, and most definitely, she must take the role of a wonder woman. She is expected to know how to successfully juggle work, family, and ministry without experiencing any exhaustion, discouragement, or pain. Have you ever found such a woman? If you have, I would most certainly like to meet her! The reality is that in this world there is no such thing as a perfect woman. As humans, we all have flaws and imperfections.

However, long ago there existed a perfect woman. She was created as a "perfect 10" and made with a perfect body.

This particular woman never knew what it felt like to go on a diet or live off of Slim Fast. She never had to spend hundreds of dollars on beauty products, because her face was wrinkle free, radiant, and stunning. She also never knew what it was to suffer from PMS, water retention, or any kind of pain. She would have been the envy of all women today. This woman was God's ultimate masterpiece. She was the very first true wonder woman on earth. We all know her as Eve. The Lord made her beautiful and flawless in every aspect of her being.

Allow me to take you on a journey into the past as we explore the origins of Eve and her husband, Adam. As we study Eve's creation, her purpose, and her mistakes, we will observe how her sin devastated her life and her relationships with her husband and her Creator, and how her image and privileges deteriorated. In doing so, we will better understand why the original sin still affects our world today. We will also learn valuable lessons from Eve's wrong doings.

Eve, the First True Wonder Woman

Let's begin by exploring what the Bible tells us about the first true wonder woman. After the fall of mankind, Adam named his wife Eve... (Gen. 3:20). The Hebrew word for Eve is *ḥăw·wā(h)*, which means *life*.[1] "Adam explains why she is named Eve. She is the 'mother of all living,' for all human life will have its source in her body. This assumes a prodigious posterity, and it is a tribute to Adam's faith in the prospect that God had revealed (vv. 15–16)."[2] Why was this woman such a wonder? First of all, she was created in a miraculous way. A synonym for the word *wonder* is *miracle*. Eve was not just a wonder, she was a miracle! Amazingly, she was the only woman on earth who was made out of a man's rib by the hand of God; she was not birthed by a woman (Gen. 2:22). Second, Eve was made pure, without any sin. Third, her body was not made to experience hardships in pregnancy and labor pains. Fourth, Eve had a true identity and was made beautiful in God's image.

Fifth, she was a wonder of a woman because she enjoyed fellowship with her Creator and was able to speak with Him directly. The Bible tells us that the Lord was walking in the garden (Gen. 3:8). What does this mean? Theologically speaking, K. A. Mathews, in the *New American Commentary*, helps us to understand what it meant for God to walk in the Garden of Eden in this quote: "The anthropomorphic description of God 'walking' (mithallēk) in the garden suggests the enjoyment of fellowship between him and our first parents."[3] *Anthropomorphic* means "the attribution of a human form, human characteristics, or human behavior to nonhuman things," and the word *mithallek* is a Hebrew word that means "*to walk or to come*." This means that God often visited Eve's "hometown" although the Bible doesn't say, it could have been in a physical form, which allow communion, as well as a great friendship.

What an honor Eve had to be able to both talk and walk with her divine Creator in a most intimate way! I can picture Eve conversing with the Lord as they strolled around the garden. I can imagine her sitting by his side on the green pastures, contemplating His presence and asking Him questions about the purposes of her duties and of her life. She was truly privileged to have had this marvelous experience. I believe that the Lord's purpose was for Eve to live eternally in His presence, praising and worshiping Him; this is the sixth and final reason I believe that Eve was such a wonder. If she had not disobeyed His command, sin and death would have never gotten in the way, and she and her offspring would have lived forever. This means that she would have never experienced a spiritual separation from God and a physical death. This and the other five factors mentioned previously illustrate why Eve was the very first true wonder woman of the Lord's creation.

Adam's Response to Eve's Creation

God had created a beautiful paradise for Adam and a variety of animals to keep him company, but obviously there was something missing in his life. The Lord felt his loneliness and realized the need for someone of Adam's own kind that could fill the gap in his heart. The Bible describes the miraculous creation of Eve: "So the Lord God caused the man to fall into a deep sleep; and while he was sleeping, he took one of the man's ribs and then closed up the place with flesh. Then the Lord God made a woman from the rib he had taken out of the man, and he brought her to the man" (Gen. 2:21-22).

Let us analyze Adam's response after seeing the very first true wonder woman ever created on earth by a majestic God. When the Lord introduced Eve to Adam, in my humble opinion, I daresay that it was love at first sight. He had never seen a female of his kind. I can imagine Adam being blown away by this marvelous woman standing right in front of him. After taking a good look at this gorgeous creature, a crown of God's creation, made with all of His splendor and beauty, Adam must have felt a tremendous sense of astonishment. Why was his heart so excited? First of all, he recognized that the Lord had provided him with a human being that was created from one of his body parts (his rib) and was a portion of him. In verse 23, we can observe that he calls her "... bone of my bones and flesh of my flesh." This meant that they were destined to be one in heart, mind, and spirit, and were intended to be soul mates.

Secondly, before the fall, he named her Woman. I often wondered why he did not name her Claudia, Elizabeth, or any other feminine name. The word woman in Hebrew is *"ishshah /ish·shaw"*, meaning *wife*.[4] By calling her ishshah, he was joyfully affirming his love for her, and was declaring his lifetime covenant to her. As his wife, she would be treated with equality, respect and honor. Adam's response toward Eve leads me to believe that he was very happy and satisfied with her. His intentions were to fully relish her companionship and make her a lifetime partner.

From Glory to Ashes

The Lord made man and woman beautiful and intelligent human beings, and He was delighted with His creation (Gen. 1:31). He also made a perfect, peaceful, and beautiful world for them to enjoy and live in happily ever after. But what happened to that wonderful ever after? Did this wonder woman and her hubby have a happy ending? At the beginning of time, God's purpose for Adam and Eve was for them to take pleasure in His holy presence in all the fullness of His glory, which included an abundance of peace, joy, and prosperity in every aspect of their lives. How cool was that? Every minute lived in utopia was to be enjoyed in ampleness. Can you picture yourself in this heavenly place, speaking to God, contemplating His magnificent presence and getting lost in all of His wonder?

As a woman, can you imagine giving birth without any pain? Eve was not meant to experience pain when giving birth. God also intended that she enjoy a drama-free and loving relationship with her husband and with Him. However, when Adam and Eve fell in disobedience by eating the fruit from the forbidden tree, this wonder- couple's time in paradise came to a halt (Gen. 3:1-6). Sin came in and produced major devastation in their lives, causing their glory to turn into ashes.

Who's to Blame?

When some people debate the subject of the original sin committed by the first human beings ever created, they automatically blame the woman. I would like to take this moment to humbly share my personal thoughts on this theological argument of who's to blame for the fall of mankind. The apostle Paul affirms in the Scriptures that Eve was the one to be deceived by the serpent to eat the fruit of the forbidden tree (1Tim.2:14).

When Adam was confronted by God for this wrongful doing, he was not a happy camper. He was angry at his wife. It seemed that this wonder woman truly messed up, and, at that moment, she was not his favorite person (you can read about Adam's accusations of Eve in (Gen. 3:12).Surely, I can understand Adam for being upset with his wife, but please let's not throw all the responsibility or blame on Eve. Allow me to say that, frankly, I do not recall any Scriptural evidence that she forced her husband to take a bite or that she threatened him by saying, "Honey, if you do not eat of this fruit, I'll have you sleeping in the dog house tonight!" On the contrary, we find in (Gen.3:6) that Adam was standing right beside her at the time that she ate the fruit: "...She took some and ate it. She also gave some to her husband, **who was with her**, and he ate it" [emphasis added].

Why didn't Adam stop Eve? After all, he was the first one to be commanded by God not to eat of the forbidden fruit (Gen. 2:16-17). In this case, I think that he, as the priest of the home, should have made an attempt to stop her from eating the fruit by firmly telling her the following: "No, honey, let's not do this. Let us obey God's orders!" Instead, he made the decision to give in. As a result, they both entered into a state of disobedience, and sin came into the human race. The consequence of their sin was catastrophic, to say the least.

The Effects of Sin

Eve had a special place and honor in paradise, but sin tore it all away, causing great havoc for this first wonder woman. Let us take a look at how sin affected Eve and the rest of us. Sin distorted Adam's view of his wife. After the fall of mankind, we can observe Adam, who was supposed to be the loving husband and protector of his beautiful wife, taking a different attitude toward her. The book of Genesis reveals a changed Adam. He is no longer joyfully praising Eve, calling her *ish-shaw* with excitement, but rather, he refers to her with a nature of resentment, blame, and guilt. His approach was to blame God for his mistakes. It seemed as if he did not want to take any responsibility for his own actions or accept any kind of accountability. With reproach, he declares: "the woman you put here with me—she gave me some fruit from the tree, and I ate it" (Gen. 3:12).

Because of his tone, we are led to believe that perhaps he was indicating that this bad situation would not have happened if God had not created a person called *woman* in the first place. I know, based upon an honest and realistic examination of the narrative of the Bible, that God was not pleased about His creation falling into sin, but in His infinite mercy, He had a plan B in mind for our redemption. Our mighty and awesome Heavenly Father never makes mistakes. Creating a woman was always in His eternal plans. Eve was not only meant to be a helper to man but also a vehicle that would be utilized to bring forth salvation to this world. It was through a woman that Jesus, our Lord and Savior, was born, in order to set all humanity free from sin and from spiritual death (Matt. 1:21).

Because of sin, Eve was condemned to experience childbirth with great pain. She was also sentenced to be subject to her husband. Sin, too, had taken away her authority and self-esteem, lowering her to become a second-class citizen. Not only was her marriage affected by sin, but, also, one of the most devastating consequences that Eve suffered was that her relationship with her Creator was broken. She no longer could speak directly with God. Due to her iniquity, she had experienced a spiritual separation from her Creator. Lastly, she would also face a physical death. Sin had stripped her from being able to live eternally.

This first wonder woman was created in the fullness of God's glory, but her sin covered her with shame and ashes. Sin ruined Eve's life. It had deteriorated the image of God in her and stripped her of all her God-given powers and strengths.

Consequences to Child Birthing

As a result of Eve's disobedience, God sentenced this first wonder woman to a life of painful childbirth experiences: "To the woman he said, 'I will surely multiply your pain in childbearing; in pain you shall bring forth children...'" (Gen.3:16a, ESV). W. D. Reyburn and E. M. Fry, in their book *A Handbook of Genesis*, help us to better understand this passage. I very much agree with their explanation concerning painful child birthing:

> **"I will greatly multiply your pain in childbearing."** This is not in the form of a curse, as in the case of the snake, although the content has the effect of a curse. **Greatly multiply** translates a Hebrew intensive construction: "I will very much increase, make worse your pain." **Pain** translates a word meaning "trouble, difficulty, labor." **Childbearing** is literally "conception." The focus is not upon the act of conception but rather upon the state of pregnancy, and so FRCL [VERSION] has "I will make your pregnancies painful," and TEV "... increase your trouble in pregnancy." **In pain you shall bring forth children**: the word **pain** is the same as above. Here, however, the reference is to labor pains that accompany childbirth, and these are represented as punishment for the woman's disobedience. In translation the words for **pain** in both clauses

should be terms associated with pregnancy and labor pains [emphasis in original].[5]

I imagine that before Eve sinned, her pregnancies were to be a piece of cake and a wonderful experience filled with great joy. However, because of sin, her pregnancies were to involve great consequences and difficulties. She would have to endure such discomforts as morning sickness, nausea, back pains, migraines, dizziness, high blood pressure, water retention, hormonal imbalance, trouble sleeping, heartburn, and so many other complications that can happen during a pregnancy. Not only would she suffer during her pregnancies, but she would also have painful deliveries. In addition, there would be a risk of her experiencing the loss of a baby or even her own life while giving birth, and the potential that her baby could be born with an illness. Her sin caused her to suffer all these complications and more when birthing her child.

The bad news for us is that the effects of her sin affected us all. Her bad became our bad. When I was pregnant with my first daughter, I had a difficult pregnancy. I experienced nine months of "morning sickness," which included vomiting, dizzy spells and other complications. As I was reaching the end of my pregnancy, I received a phone call from a brother in Christ. His purpose was to encourage me and prepare me mentally to deal with labor pains. He reassured me with these words: "Evie, I know that this is your first baby, and you do not have experience in this matter. But I want you to know that because you are a child of God and you are now living in the time of grace, you will not experience any pain while giving birth, and if pain comes, you must rebuke it." I was very naïve at that time, so I believed him. When the time arrived for giving birth and those so-called labor pains kicked in, reality hit me with a vengeance. In that moment, I remembered that dear brother and started thinking all sorts of bad things about him in my mind, things that I will not repeat because I do not wish to sin again. I focused my attention on my husband; I held his hand very tight and kept repeating to him, "I hate Mickey Mouse!"

I also thought about Eve, and, yes, I must confess that I wished she was standing in my presence so I could give her a piece of my mind. In that particular instant, I visualized a pretend scenario in which God was placing Eve in a protection witness program up in heaven with the purpose of keeping her safe and alive. I do not think that she is a celebrity among women who are in labor pain. Of course, when all was said and done, I realized that the pains of child birthing is simply a reminder to us women of Eve's consequences and of an inherited fallen nature that will ultimately change when we get to heaven. I asked the Lord for forgiveness, and He replied, "You must have a forgiving heart." I forgave Eve and the brother who totally got his facts wrong about women experiencing labor pains.

After the whole trial of giving birth was over, I was more relaxed. While holding my beautiful daughter in my arms, my husband asked me, "Why were you screaming 'I hate Mickey Mouse'?" I replied, "I was having the worst contractions, and I could not bear the pain. At that moment, I wanted to say *I hate you,* but you were being very nice to me. I needed to take it out on someone else, and Mickey Mouse was the first thing that popped into my head. But do not get me wrong, I still like you and Mickey Mouse, too." We women say the craziest things while giving birth!

Women Were Placed in a State of Subjection

Genesis 3:16b records that the Lord not only sentenced Eve to painful child birthing but also finished pronouncing his judgment toward her. He said: "Your desire will be for your husband, and he will rule over you". Eve would now be subject to her husband. For this topic, we will analyze the following: What does it mean to be subject to someone? How did sin distort the attitude toward this position and what does His Word reveal about how godly wives are to behave toward their husbands? What does it reveal about how husbands ought to treat their wives?

The Merriam-Webster Dictionary defines the word *subject* as one who is placed under authority or control. When we read this end-part of Eve's sentence of being ruled by her husband, for some women, it feels as if God was unfair. To them, being subject to one's husband feels like a punishment. Was this judgment meant to be a curse or a blessing in disguise? What do you think? Although I have a Master's in Theology, I do not claim to be a theologian or a scholar. However, I would like to give my humble opinion of what God meant in this particular Bible verse. I would also like to explain how sin altered a godly attitude toward subjection between a husband and wife.

Sin Distorted a Godly Attitude toward Subjection

To fully understand God's judgement toward Eve concerning her husband ruling over her, we must turn to the Holy Scriptures and see the order in which the Lord made all things. Man was created first (Gen. 2:7). God placed him in the Garden of Eden to oversee it, and put him in charge of naming the animals and caring for them. Then He realized that the man was lonely and needed someone to help him with his duties. God said in verse 18, "It is not good for the man to be alone. I will make a helper suitable for him." Since the man was made first, he was meant to be the priest of his home and therefore care for his wife.

Before the fall, this wonder couple had a blissful marriage. There was peace and harmony in their relationship and pride did not exist between them. They lived only to please God and to please themselves with an unselfish love. Eve had no problem subjecting herself to her husband: therefore, God did not have to enforce any laws concerning the chain of authority in the marriage. Adam and Eve knew their places: Adam was the head of the home, and Eve was his helper. They both respected their positions. However, when sin entered into the human race, men's and women's godly natures turned into worldly natures, producing selfishness, self-centeredness, pride, arrogance, and many other ungodly carnal fruits.

When Eve gave into temptation, sin distorted her attitude toward her husband. What did it mean when God told her, "Your desire will be for your husband" (Gen. 3:16)? J. Swanson in his *Dictionary of Biblical Languages,* defines the root word for *desire* in Hebrew as $t^e š û\cdot q ā(h)$, which means, "a very strong emotion or feeling to have or do something. (Gen. 3:16; 4:7) note: this strong desire may refer to sexual urges or desires, or a desire to dominate, or just be independent of the man."[6] My mind is blown away as I try to understand Swanson's comparison between Eve and Cain. He compares Eve's desire for her husband (Gen. 3:16) to when God told Cain that "...sin is crouching at the door. Its desire is for you, but you must rule over it." (Gen. 4:7). Sin was longing and desiring to control Cain, but he was too weak and allowed sin to take him over. As a consequence, he killed his younger brother. In the same manner, because sin took over Eve's human nature, she would find herself vulnerable, and sin would be crouching at her door, constantly demanding for her to want to dominate her husband.

As Eve's heart was taken over by sin, the Lord knew that it was going to be a challenge for her to be subject to her husband. There was going to be a power struggle between them. When God was sentencing her, He was establishing a new order of authority in marriage. Things would now change for Eve. As a married woman, she had to be accountable solely to her husband. I believe that God's sentence to the woman was meant to be a merciful act of grace and provision for her. Now that sin had been born into mankind, it had the power to destroy her—there's no telling what it could do to her. The Lord knew that she needed a strong man to protect her from the beguiling acts of sin, and that is why Eve was sentenced to be ruled by her husband.

The Bible does not specifically include the following words, but this is how I picture God explaining to Eve why Adam was to rule over her: "Listen Eve, I am not pleased with what you did. When you disobeyed my command, you invited sin to come into your life and into the world. You have no idea what kind of monster you have unleashed. Sin destroys everything in its path. I always enjoyed your company and talking with you face to face, but because of sin, not only was our bond broken and you will bear your children with pain, but also sin has just altered your state of independence.

You cannot come and go as you please. Your husband will rule over you to protect you. I am a Holy God and sin cannot abide in my home; therefore, you and your husband will be sent into exile in a hostile land that will be affected by sin. Sin can create serious consequences in your life. It will try to lead you onto a darker path, causing you to do malicious things. Sin will also try to seduce you into manipulating and dominating your husband; in addition, it can take you further to hurt him emotionally, spiritually, financially, and even physically, if you allow it to rule over you. It can make you weak; so I am assigning your husband to oversee you, help you in all things, guide you with wisdom, protect you, and provide for you. He must make sure that you have a roof over your head and food on your table, and he must love you and treat you with respect. He will continue to be the priest of your home, and you will submit to him."

When God allowed Adam to rule over his wife, He did not command him to boss her around, bully her, and mistreat her. I believe that the Lord's intention was for Adam to rule over her with love and respect. However, sin also changed Adam's attitude toward his wife. He could choose to do as sin might lead him to do, concerning how to rule over her. When a husband rules over his wife under the influence of sin and Satan, it is most likely that he will treat her unkindly and foolishly. As a result, his wife will respond with hostility. Likewise, when a wife allows her sinful nature to take over, she most likely will act in rebellion toward her spouse. Mathew Henry, in *Matthew Henry's Commentary on the Whole Bible*, gives his opinion on how sin affected Adam and Eve's marriage regarding ruling and subjection. "The entrance of sin has made that duty a punishment, which otherwise it would not have been. If man had not sinned, he would always have ruled with wisdom and love; and, if the woman had not sinned, she would always have obeyed with humility and meekness; and then the dominion would have been no grievance."[7] Sin totally changed their attitudes toward one another. Allow me to reiterate that if sin had not come into their lives, Adam would have continued to treat his wife with respect, love, and equality. In the same manner, Eve would not have had any problems submitting to her husband.

The Bible urges women to submit to their spouses, but it also clearly says that husbands are to be thoughtful, caring, and understanding toward their wives. In the book of 1 Peter, the apostle Peter commands husbands to be considerate with their wives and to treat them with respect and honor as the weaker vessel (1 Pet. 3:7). The Greek word for *weak* is *astenes,* meaning *physically weak*.[8] The apostle Peter is recognizing that men are physically stronger than women are when it comes to picking up heavier objects; however, he is not suggesting that women are less than or inferior to men. This does not give the husband the right to mistreat his wife. It simply means that, as the weaker vessel, the wife can be in need of assistance and care. When the Lord gave out the new commands to Eve to submit, He did it because He knew that she needed a strong man by her side to help her with difficult tasks. She also needed a husband to be the head of her home and the commander of her ship. He was not to oppress her but rather treat her with kindness. I agree with Mathew Henry about how a husband ought to treat his wife. He says that, "The woman was *made of a rib out of the side of Adam* [emphasis in the original]; not made out of his head to rule over him, nor out of his feet to be trampled upon by him, but out of his side to be equal with him, under his arm to be protected, and near his heart to be beloved."[9] Adam, as Eve's husband, was to protect her in their new dreadful environment: spiritually, from the deceitfulness of the enemy, and also physically, from the evils of the world. Although the Lord was saddened and disappointed by Eve's fall, in spite of it all, He loved her. He left her with a command that seemed like a punishment, but as I said before, it signified an act of grace.

After the fall, sin turned the act of subjection of a wife to her husband to be more like a burden or retribution. Once again, I agree with Mathew Henry as he declares, "Our own sin and folly make our yoke heavy."[10] Our sinful attitudes toward being subject to our husbands can lead us to act foolishly, and this can become a heavy burden. You might say, "Well, my husband does not deserve for me to be subject to him." Allow me to respond. If he does not comply with God's Word, he will be accountable to the Lord for his actions toward you. I would also like to add that if your husband is trying to make you live a life that is not according to God's Word, it is important that you seek Godly counsel from your pastor or minister. Continue praying for your husband and remember the apostle Peter's advice to wives married to unbelievers: "Wives, in the same way submit yourselves to your own husbands so that, if any of them do not believe the word, they may be won over without words by the behavior of their wives when they see the purity and reverence of your lives" (1 Pt. 3:1-2).

God's Word on Subjection

What does the Word of God continue to teach us concerning being subject to our husbands? The apostle Paul advised the Christian women of the city of Ephesus and all the women of today by saying: "Wives submit yourselves to your own husbands as you do to the Lord" (Eph.5:22). Just as Jesus set the ultimate example of submission to a higher power, we ought to do the same to our husbands. To Jesus, it wasn't a punishment or a heavy burden to submit His will to His Heavenly Father. He simply did it because He loved Him with all of His heart. If we love our husbands with a godly and pure love, it will not be a burden to allow them to exercise their God-given role in the family. When doing this, we are also submitting to Christ our Lord. Jesus surrendered to the Father by subjecting himself to the cross and death, and, as a result, the Father exalted Him to His Glory (Phil. 2:7-9).

We can experience peace and harmony in our homes, and love, respect and exaltation from our husbands when we submit to them in a godly way. I would like to clarify that submitting to our husbands does not imply that we are to be their slaves; it simply means that we ought to give our husbands their place as the priest of our household, all while knowing our position in the home. God is pleased when we follow His Word and commands. As a result of our obedience to His Word, the yoke that sin has placed on subjection becomes lighter, and we are filled with joy.

Mrs. Mary Elizabeth Baxter speaks about a case of a prudent and unselfish wife that knew how to get her husband's affection. She says,

"One of the happiest marriages we know was entered into by a dear Christian woman on the Continent with a blind minister for the very purpose of caring for him. Being eyes to him, she enables him to carry out his ministerial work. Why is it so happy? Because it is unselfish; she is a helpmeet for her husband, and she has found in him patience and a self-denial which, with her naturally impetuous and impulsive disposition, makes the gain as much hers as his. When a wife seeks in her husband the affection which shall satisfy her, or the attention which shall gratify her self-love, she is not acting as a helpmate; she is making her husband minister to her, instead of taking her place as minister to him. And when a husband is exacting with his wife, claiming all her time, all her attention, all her thoughts to revolve around him, he will never be fully satisfied with her. Selfishness is a plant that produces sour fruit, and sows discord wherever it grows."[11]

This story is a great example of how a godly woman handles the effects of sin and subjection toward her husband. Because of sin, the first wonder woman was sentenced to a life of subjection to her husband, and that judgment affected all women. With a sinful attitude, subjection can become a burden, and it can hold its tightest grip when we are prideful, selfish, and unwilling to serve our husbands with love. Therefore, with God's power and grace, we too can overcome sin and learn how to submit to His Holy Word and to our husbands. In doing so, we live as the true wonder women God called us to be.

Sin Degraded Women

In many parts of the world, due to sin, evil men have taken away women's freedom and voice. They have considered them as second-class citizens. Women have been subjected to violence, slavery, harsh abuse; they have been utilized as sex objects, and have been degraded to the core. There are cultures and countries that commit horrendous acts of violence toward them. In the United States, women are not exempt from such acts and from experiencing abuse in different ways. There are a high percentage of women in this country who have suffered verbal, emotional, and physical abuse such as rape, kidnapping, domestic violence, and even death.

I knew a woman named Sheila. She was a hard-working mother of three children who lived with an alcoholic husband who physically abused her. One terrible evening, they got into an argument, and her husband began to beat her. He broke her arms and ribs. His intention was to kill her. The neighbor heard her screams and called the police. She was taken immediately to the hospital, and her husband was taken into custody. With the help of a professional spiritual counselor, she found the courage to abandon that relationship for the safety of her children and for her own. I admire Sheila for being bold enough to leave that abusive relationship that almost took her life. Women who are in that same predicament often find it hard to leave an abuser because of low self-esteem, guilt, shame, or fear. The emotional wounds they have endured are too deep and have made them feel that they cannot make it on their own. I am not an expert in this field, but if you are experiencing abuse, I would like to give you some words of encouragement.

If you are a victim of domestic violence, I would like you to know that there is a God that loves you and does not wish to see you suffer such abuse. It is the enemy's goal to destroy you emotionally, spiritually, and physically. The Psalmist encourages us to call upon the Lord for help (**Ps. 34:6**). God will always give you a way out and give you the courage to move out of your harmful place. If your life is in danger from an abusive relationship, I recommend that you seek both professional and spiritual counselors for support. If needed, they can lead you to a woman's shelter.

Learning from Eve's Mistakes

What lessons can we learn from this wonder woman called Eve? She was made perfect, sinless and in God's image alongside her husband. There was supposed to be a happily ever after for this twosome in the Garden. What went wrong? It all began when Eve interacted with the serpent that was being utilized by Satan to tempt her (Gen. 3:1-5). As we go back to this scene, I will present some lessons to learn from Eve's mistakes that led her to fall.

Never Lend an Ear to the Devil

Jesus clearly revealed the truth concerning Satan's character in (Jn.8:44). The devil is a liar and a deceiver. He was called a murderer from the beginning: a liar, and a father of all lies. His words deceived and killed the essence of God's truth in the mind of Eve. The conversation between Eve and the serpent in the Garden of Eden made way for her to distrust her Creator and ultimately disobey the Lord. The devil was sowing seeds of suspicion and doubt in her mind.

The proposed question from the serpent to Eve was nothing short of a direct attack on God and on His laws for Adam and Eve. The more we lend an ear to Satan, the closer we are to believing his lies and can be easily deceived if our faith in God is not strong enough. It is the devil's goal to discredit the Lord's Word. The Bible tells us that the enemy makes it his priority to steal the seed that has been planted by God's Word in the hearts of men (Mrk.4:15).

Sometimes the devil comes to us in the midst of our Eden or perfect place to disturb our minds and cause us to doubt God's promises. I too had a moment when I let my guard down and my Eden was disturbed. Allow me to share this story. In 2006, I was about to receive a Master's degree in Theology from Vanguard University, but before graduation, I needed to pay off a balance of one thousand dollars to the school. I did not have the money or any other financial resources. I had a moment of vulnerability, and my faith began to be shaken. The enemy took the opportunity to speak lies into my head. He enticed me by posing dubious questions such as, "Where is your God now? Has He abandoned you?" All of a sudden, I found myself talking back to him. I responded, "You know, I think you may be right." Allowing these thoughts to wander too long in my mind caused very real doubt and fear; however, the Lord in his mercy reached out to me and supplied me the money in a miraculous way. Someone anonymously donated the money and paid off my balance. I praise the Lord for His kindness and merciful acts toward this unworthy servant.

I personally have learned lessons from my shortcomings. I learned that I should never allow myself to listen to the enemy's lies or consider his deceiving thoughts, and at no time should I allow my faith in God to waver. I can testify that, throughout my life, God has never failed me. I know that His Word is true when He says, "He will not fail thee, neither forsake thee; fear not, neither be dismayed" (Deut. 31:8, KJV).

Reject the Negative Thoughts

As Satan was planting his deceitful words in Eve's mind regarding God's commands for her, she payed attention to his words without correctly recognizing them as deceptive. For an instant, she ignored how much the Lord loved her and how much He had blessed her by giving her all the benefits of the divine place called The Garden of Eden. She lived in an environment where everything around her was pure, lovely, admirable, excellent, and praiseworthy. She did not think about such right things or any future consequences. As she gave attention to the serpent's words, she allowed herself to be misled about God's truth.

It is the enemy's mission to twist God's truth and misguide us into his web of lies, but how can we avoid the negative thoughts that enter our minds? Martin Luther is reported to have said, "You can't stop a bird from flying over your head, but you can stop it from making a nest in your hair."[12] We cannot avoid Satan's negative thoughts, which fly into our heads like darts, but we can reject them in Jesus' name. He has given us the authority to do so. The apostle Paul, in his letter to the Philippians, reveals a powerful tool that empowers us to discard the devil's lies and opposing thoughts. This tool can be used as a formula for casting out all wrongful, deceptive thoughts. He says, "Finally, brothers and sisters, whatever is true, whatever is noble, whatever is right, whatever is pure, whatever is lovely, whatever is admirable—if anything is excellent or praiseworthy—think about such things" (Phil. 4:8).

The next time the enemy tries to entice you with deceitful thoughts, turn it around and think about the truth of God's Word, for it is His truth that will set you free (Jn. 8:32). In addition, think how noble, right, pure, and lovely is the Lord's purpose for your life. Experience His magnificent presence, which is excellent and praiseworthy. When you allow your mind to be saturated with Christ's power and when you understand that you have "the mind of Christ," there will be no room for Satan's lies to penetrate and pollute your mind (1 Cor. 2:16).

Guard Your God-Given Senses

God has graciously blessed the human body with five senses: sight, hearing, taste, smell and touch. Because of these senses, we enjoy being able to see all the beauty that God has created, to hear and touch our loved ones, and to smell and taste good food. It is His pleasure that we appreciate these senses and utilize them in a godly way. Satan's intention is to lure us into surrendering our God-given senses to his evil ways with the purpose of destroying our faith in God, and causing us to stumble into spiritual darkness. That is what the devil did to Eve. He seduced her into using her five senses for the wrong reason, which ultimately caused her to sin against God.

The Lord forbade Adam and Eve to eat any fruit from the tree of knowledge of good and evil. God had planted this particular tree in the middle of the garden (Gen. 2:9). It was surrounded by other trees that also produced edible fruit, which they were allowed to eat. Eve must have passed by this forbidden tree many times without giving much thought to it. However, as soon as the serpent began to speak to her with his seductive manner, he tapped into her human senses, arousing curiosity in her to look further into this particular tree. This wonder woman left her God-given senses unguarded. As she heard the enemy's voice, she allowed her sense of hearing to be vulnerable to deception. Eve was a woman who had the privilege of hearing God's voice speak to her frequently. Sadly, she took Him for granted and instead chose to listen to the deceiver. The Lord is real, and He longs to speak to us. His voice is accessible through His Spirit and also through His Word. Like Eve, we have the option of choosing whose voice we are going to listen to. If we decide to listen to the Holy Spirit, He will guide us to find eternal life in Christ; however, if we choose to listen to that old serpent, just as he did to Eve, he will lead us astray to live a life of spiritual brokenness and condemnation.

The second sense the enemy tapped into was the sense of sight, mentioned in the book of Genesis. It says, "When the woman *saw* [emphasis added]" (Gen. 3:6). The word *saw* in Hebrew is *ra'ah*/raw·**aw**, which means to learn about, inspect, and find out.[13] As Eve surrendered her sense of sight to the enemy's will, the forbidden fruit now seemed to be more appealing, and it led her to have a strong desire to inspect, get close to, and learn about this fruit. The forbidden fruit is always most striking to the eye. Let us be aware and never ignore the fact that the devil will not tempt us with something that is ugly and unattractive in our sight, but rather he presents and dresses up all of his temptations in a provocative and appealing form. As Eve reached for and ate the forbidden fruit, not only were her senses of hearing and sight seduced but also her senses of smell, touch, and taste were led astray. Leaving all her senses unguarded and giving into temptation caused her spiritual and physical death. If we want to enjoy perpetual fellowship with God, then it is imperative to guard our God-given senses and yield them to the Holy Spirit instead of surrendering them to Satan's deceit.

Run from Temptation

In this world, we will all suffer trials and temptations. It is important to understand that one does not sin by being tempted. The Bible clearly says that we are blessed when we resist temptation. Temptation of itself is not a sin. Temptation becomes a sin in our lives only when we give into it (Jm. 1:12). How can we avoid falling into temptation? As we mentioned previously, the first wonder woman of the Bible, Eve, was not only tempted but gave into temptation. Had she taken a godly and wise approach by ignoring Satan's enticement, she could have had a successful encounter against temptation. The outcome of her story would have been different.

The Bible tells of a great character named Joseph (son of Jacob). He teaches us a lesson on what to do whenever we face temptation. Joseph found himself tempted by his boss' wife. As she tried to seduce him into sleeping with her, he quickly ran out of her presence (Gen. 39:12). When we are facing temptation, Joseph's example teaches us that it is best not to stick around but rather run from it as fast as we can.

Be Satisfied with All That God Has Given You

Eve was made in the image of God and lived out a wonderful relationship with her Creator. She was married to her prince charming and lived in an amazing and beautiful land. It was created especially for her and her spouse. She was also given power to be the queen and rule over all creatures alongside her husband in their kingdom, the Garden of Eden (Gen.1:26-27). Apparently, all the heavenly comforts were not enough to satisfy this first wonder woman. Most people are not satisfied with the wonderful things that the Lord places in their hands. We always strive for more, especially for power. We learn from the Bible that we must be happy with all that God has given us, as indicated in **(Heb.13:5)**, "... Be content with what you have..."

Eve had everything a woman could possibly dream of, and still she was not pleased. What motivated her to want more? I believe that the serpent was insinuating to Eve that the Creator was selfish and inconsiderate in not wanting to share His wisdom with her. His enticing words made her feel that the Lord was trying to keep her from tapping into greater power that would allow her to be more than just His creation and a helper to Adam, but would enable her to obtain a greater wisdom that only God possessed: "When the woman saw that the fruit of the tree was good for food and pleasing to the eye, and also desirable for gaining wisdom..."(Gen. 3:6). The word *desirable* in Hebrew is *ḥā·măḏ*, which means to covet, lust, or strongly desire another's possessions.[14] As

Eve believed the serpent's words, I can picture her eyes being blinded by covetousness and lust, which motivated her to seek more than what was given to her.

We can sit around all day judging Eve, but we are sometimes as guilty as she when we allow Satan to fill our hearts with worldly ambitions that will only lead us into living a life of spiritual poverty. If you ever find yourself in a situation where Satan is luring you into lusting or desiring forbidden fruit, before you give into it, think about the consequences that can devastate your world. We are told to resist the enemy and to be thankful and satisfied with all that God has given us. When the Lord blesses us, He never leaves us in a state of want or need; when He blesses, He does it abundantly.

God Is a God of Redemption

The Bible does not speak much about the life of Eve after the fall, but she is mentioned in verses 1, 2, and 25 of the fourth chapter of Genesis, when she gives birth to Cain, Abel, and Seth. I can imagine Eve feeling sorry and repentant for her disobedience. Reading these verses, we see a changed Eve. She is no longer a woman pursuing independence from her Creator; on the contrary, her sinful and weak human condition has made her realize how much she needs His strength. Considering the fact that child birthing was a challenge, she acknowledges that it was only through God's help that she was able to birth a child. She had learned to completely depend on her Heavenly Father. She suffered the loss of her second child, but nonetheless experienced the Lord's mercy and provision. He gave her another son; showing her that He loved her.

In spite of our sins, the Lord's love is endless and merciful toward his children. Our God is a God of redemption who believes in restoring what is broken. Although sin affected the human race, it did not have the last say. The Lord had prepared a plan for redemption and restoration for women and for all humanity.

Conclusion

Eve was the very first true wonder woman to be created on earth in a miraculous way. She was given extraordinary privileges, but she lost them all because of her sin. Sin not only affected her life but also spread to all mankind, causing major consequences. Although sin is still active and present in this world, we do not have to live bound by it. Through the power of the Holy Spirit, we can rise above and overcome the temptations of this world, say no to sin, and stand against Satan. Today, God wants to equip you with His mighty power. All you have to do is call upon His name. I invite you to join me in this prayer, asking for His power to overcome Satan's temptations in your life.

Prayer for Power

Dear Heavenly Father, thank You for creating me in Your image. Although sin devastated the first wonder woman and the human race, from the beginning You had a master plan for the restoration of mankind. Before the foundations of the earth were laid, You thought about me. You have designed a special blueprint with my name on it, so that I may construct boundless and mighty things in Your name for Your honor and glory. I declare that sin will not take hold of me but that the all-consuming fire of Your Holy Spirit will embrace and empower me to love and serve You. May Your Spirit continue working in me, leading me into a journey of discovering that marvelous true wonder woman that You intend me to become. I pray that You will fill me continuously with wisdom and power in order to overcome all the temptations that may come my way. Thank You my Heavenly Father. In Jesus' name I pray. Amen.

Chapter Two

The former glory of the first wonder woman was deteriorated by sin, but through Jesus Christ, all women have been restored to a greater Honor & Power.

Elevating the True Wonder Woman to His Glory

"*When I was young, like any other little girl, I dreamed of someday becoming a princess. There were days when I fantasized for hours of how I would be swept away by a prince charming and how he would take me to a faraway country to live in a beautiful castle. But something happened along the way that shattered all my dreams. My soul was left in ruins by my past sins. I still do not understand how I got there; I guess I was looking for love in all the wrong places. I wish I could have made better choices, but as of now I'm stuck in a rut. It's morning time and I am in need of water. My jar is empty, but I think I'm going to wait until*

later to fetch some at the well. I do not want to run into the people of my neighborhood, who go there in the morning to fetch water. By noon, they'll be gone and I'll have some time alone and maybe some kind of peace of mind, away from all the harassment. I prefer to avoid their gossip and criticisms. They do not like me very much. Why must they be so harsh and judgmental? They do not know how my heart has suffered and how I hurt inside. Yes, I know that in the past I've had several husbands, but those relationships did not work out. They left me poor and spiritually bankrupt. I have been searching for love but I have not been successful. As of now, I am in a new relationship. He is the number six in my life. Although I am with him, I still feel so alone; unloved and banned by everyone. I've wondered if there is anything better out there for me, but now it's too late. Are you wondering who I am? I am the woman at the well. I am also known as the Samaritan woman from the fourth chapter of the Gospel of John."

This is the story of a woman affected by sin. The Bible does not provide a narrative of her thoughts as written in the story above; but after reading about her in the Gospel of John, I am envisioning this Biblical character as if she was relating her story and expressing her feelings about the conditions she lived in. Apparently she had a bad reputation in her town for having had five husbands and living with a man that was not her actual spouse. It was most likely that she was treated as an outcast or looked upon as a prostitute. She lived a life of a broken woman who gave her body and all that she had to different people, hoping to find real love, security, provision and protection from a true man.

Was it too late for this Samaritan woman to find hope, love and a new beginning? She was not only in need of a man that would genuinely love her and provide for her; but also, she was in an extreme state of spiritual drought. She went to the well with the intentions of getting physical water. What she did not know was that on a particular day, she would find a Savior that would touch her heart with His love and compassion, and also quench her spiritual thirst. Because Jesus loved her, He took a detour to Samaria, a land where Jews were not welcomed, in order to provide for her inner needs. Jesus restored this woman's life from her ashes; elevating her to His glory. He turned her away from a life of prostitution, filled with shame and guilt, to one of a true wonder woman of God.

In biblical times, the Samaritan woman became an evangelist. She became a witness of Christ to her community (Jn. 4:39). As a result, people in her town were curious to hear all about the Son of God, and countless were saved. It is wonderful to know that whenever we might be facing a spiritual drought and in need of true love, Jesus, the lover of our souls, will show up in the common places of our lives to quench our spiritual thirst. We were all destined to die in our sins, but Christ came to bring salvation to mankind. He also came to elevate all women from their ashes to His glory and to reinstate them to a life empowered by the Holy Spirit.

Jesus showed women that, through Him, they could rise above the tyranny of sin and Satan. Through His death and resurrection, He elevated women to their rightful place as *redeemed daughters of God*. In this chapter, we will look into the lives of some women in the New Testament that were transformed and elevated to Christ's glory. We will also learn how the apostle Paul recognized the gifts and talents of some of the godly women who dared to follow Christ.

Biblical Women Who Made a Difference

There are many wonder women in the Bible who are memorialized for their good deeds. Although this chapter is not about all the women of the Bible, I would like to mention a few that stand out in my heart; these are Mary the mother of Jesus, Mary Magdalene, Mary and Martha, and other women in the New Testament. I admire them for their courage, faith, and devotion to God. These women made a difference in the world because they allowed Christ to dictate their walk in their journey of discovering the true wonder women in them. There is a lot that we can learn from them. In the previous chapter, we learned how sin in the Old Testament came through Eve, the first wonder woman, and devastated the earth. However, in the New Testament, the Lord raised a true wonder woman to give birth to a Savior that would restore our hope, salvation, and honor.

Mary, the Mother of Jesus, an Obedient Servant

The Bible says that when God sentence the serpent who caused Adam and Eve to fall, He uttered a prophetic word concerning the outcome of the seed of the woman. He said, "...He will crush your head, and you will strike his heel." (Gen.3:15). Through this prophecy, we see how God's love and mercy elevated the woman by giving her a promise of restoration. Through a woman's womb, a seed of redemption would come to earth in order to overthrow Satan's power and his entire kingdom. Through Christ, women and the rest of the world would be restored to God's glory. The gospel of Luke records the story of a young woman by the name of Mary who found favor in the eyes of God. She was a virgin and was promised to Joseph as his betrothed (Lk. 1:26-38). It was customary in biblical times for Hebrew fathers to arrange their daughters' marriages. It is believed that Mary was a teenager at the time of her engagement.

How was Mary elevated to Christ's glory? We admire Mary for her courage and obedience. When the angel told her that she was going to conceive a divine child, she said yes to His call, regardless of the consequences (v. 38). According to the Old Testament laws, if a virgin was found unfaithful to her betrothed, she would most likely be stoned to death (Deut. 28:30; 22:22; 2 Sam. 3:14). Mary's life could have been in danger; she could have been rejected by her family and friends and despised by her neighbors, but, in spite of it all, she accepted God's will and the Lord exalted her. She was called blessed among all women in the world and had the privilege of birthing the Savior of mankind (Lk. 1:42). The Bible tells us that Mary as a mother took her young son Jesus under her wing and instructed Him in the Lord's ways. She knew in her heart that He was truly the Son of God and her responsibility was to raise Him well. Scripture says: "Then he went down to Nazareth with them and was obedient to them. But His mother treasured all these things in her heart. And Jesus grew in wisdom and stature..." (Lk.2:51-52). It is amazing to know that the Lord chose a woman to nurture and care for Him as a child here on earth—and to be his mentor. Mary also believed that Jesus, as the Son of God, could perform miracles. That is why she encouraged Jesus to activate

His power when the opportunity presented itself at a wedding in Cana (Jn.2:3-5).

Mary was elevated to Christ's glory because she was an obedient servant of God. She believed and accepted Jesus as Her Lord and Savior. She also followed His ministry until His death (Jn. 19:26). What can we learn from this true wonder woman called Mary? Mary wasn't afraid to obey God's will for her. We too must not be afraid to say yes when He places a special calling in our lives. Obedience to the Lord activates a spiritual seed that ultimately will birth miracles in your life and in your ministry.

Mary Magdalene, the Devoted Servant

Throughout Jesus' ministry, the Scriptures attest to Christ's compassion for women. Many women followed Him, and Mary Magdalene was one of them (Lk. 8:2-3). She was considered to be the leader of the women who ministered to the needs of Jesus, and she supported Him and His disciples with her resources. It is believed that Mary Magdalene was a woman of financial means. Herbert Lockyer explains the meaning of her name and her background:

> "The present Mary is distinguished from all others of the same name as "The Magdalene," which identifies her with her place of birth, just as Jesus was called "The Nazarene" because of His association with Nazareth. Magdala means "tower" or "castle," and in the time of Christ was a thriving, populous town on the coast of Galilee about three miles from Capernaum. Dye works and primitive textile factories added to the wealth of

the community. It may be that "The Magdalene" was connected with the industry of the town for it would seem as if she was not without means, enabling her to serve the Lord with her substance."[15]

Mary Magdalene was tormented by seven evil spirits (Lk.8:2). As soon as Jesus came across her path, He could not help but pour His love and power over her, and ultimately, set her free from her demons. Our Lord has always been and always will be a gentle and loving God. He not only looked at Mary Magdalene with eyes of love and compassion, but He saw a potential in her to become a true wonder woman for His kingdom. After her deliverance, she became a devoted servant. Jesus had elevated her to His glory and had turned her from a life of demon possession to a life full of purpose, faith and service unto Him. She followed Christ through His death and resurrection (Mrk. 15:47). She was privileged to be the very first one to see Jesus resurrected (Mrk 16:9). Also, she was the first woman to receive the divine assignment of spreading the news to the disciples of His resurrection (Jn. 20:16-18). Mary Magdalene teaches us that devotion to Christ must be demonstrated with a heart filled with love and gratitude.

Mary and Martha, Friends of God

The Bible also speaks of two particular women who had a close relationship with the Lord Jesus Christ. Mary and Martha, along with their brother Lazarus, were considered to be His buddies. In a world where men ruled and women were considered of little worth, why would Jesus choose to have a special friendship with Mary and Martha, and how did He elevate them to His glory? In His sight, they were as important as the men. Jesus elevated them to His glory by acknowledging them as His friends. The Lord valued the friendship of women. Back in the Old Testament, because of sin, Eve's fellowship with her Creator was torn apart. In the New Testament, Jesus came to restore our broken relationship with God.

The Lord calls us friends (Jn. 15:15). Jesus loved Mary and Martha (Jn. 11:5). These women were His true wonder women. They were special to Christ because they knew how to show love and true worship unto Him. Whenever the Lord came to their town, they were hospitable to Him (Lk. 10:38). As they threw a dinner in honor of Jesus, Martha served her Lord with gladness (Jn. 12:2). Also, whenever Mary had the chance, she would throw herself at Jesus' feet to worship Him, and on one occasion, she anointed His feet (Jn. 12:3). Mary and Martha's brother became sick, and they sent word to Jesus to come to them (Jn. 11:3). Their plea was very important to Him. The Lord could have very well ignored their request, but in His time, He came. As it seemed, Lazarus had died. It was a devastating moment for these sisters, but in the midst of their loss, it was also an opportunity for them to experience a miraculous act of God.

When Jesus got there and saw how Mary and the rest were weeping, His heart was moved. He felt their pain, and He wept (Jn. 11:33, 35). When a woman hurts, He feels her pain. He encouraged Martha to believe in a miracle, for the Lord was about to show her and Mary God's glory (Jn. 11:40). Soon after, he gave them a reason not to cry anymore. He raised Lazarus from the dead, and the Lord's name was glorified. I reiterate: Jesus hurts when we are hurting, and it is His desire to comfort us in our pain. He not only brings relief in the midst of our sufferings, but also creates miracles when we believe. Allow me to share this powerful testimony of an honorable woman who, in the midst of her loss, through her faith experienced God's glory.

This is Molly's story. She is a true wonder woman in my book. One dreary day, during the Thanksgiving holiday, we received a dreadful phone call from a dear friend. In that moment, we fell into a state of shock as we discovered that Molly, a mother of two, lost her youngest child. He was twenty months old when he accidently drowned in the family's backyard pool. Molly and her family endured months of deep sadness and a sense of void from their loss, but thankfully, they remained strong in faith. The faith of an honorable woman has the power to draw Jesus to cause miracles in her life. Four and a half months later, Molly learned that she was expecting; thereafter, she was told that she was going to have twin boys. This news brought an abundant joy to the family and created a boundless gratitude in their hearts. This was nothing short of a miracle, because Molly had had a tubal ligation procedure done after having her last child. Having an operation such as this one meant that it is very difficult and usually impossible to get pregnant. In the book of Luke, Scripture encourages us that "nothing is impossible with God" (1:37). After losing her baby boy, Molly had been praying and longing for another child. She lost one son, but the Lord compensated her with two beautiful boys that filled her heart with gladness. Molly and her family praised Jesus for their miracle!

God does not expect us to understand why terrible things happen to us, such as losing a loved one, but He does expect us to trust Him in the process. He is always there to comfort us in our pain in times of grief. In times of adversity, as friends of God, we can trust that He hears our pleas and can heal our brokenness and reward our faith. Miracles will happen if we believe in our true friend, Jesus Christ.

The Apostle Paul Acknowledged Women in Ministry

When it came to women, Jesus healed their infirmities, forgave their sins, restored their self-esteem and honor, and elevated them to His glory. After He ascended to heaven, the apostle Paul continued Christ's work in raising women's worth, and carried His work further. In a world where women did not have a say, the apostle Paul recognized that godly women had tremendous potential for service in God's kingdom. He acknowledged their spiritual gifts, talents, and leadership. He also positioned them in ministry and celebrated their accomplishments in Christ's service. Such was the case for each of the following women: ***Priscilla*** was a Christian woman who lived in the city of Ephesus. She was acknowledged by the apostle Paul as having a heart for ministry and for exercising great leadership (1 Cor. 16:19). She, along with her husband, opened up her home in order to serve as a church. The apostle also mentioned how Priscilla served as a teacher and mentor to a Jew named Apollos in order to better equip him for his evangelistic ministry (Acts 18:24-26).

Another godly woman recorded in the New Testament is ***Phoebe.*** The apostle Paul encouraged the church in his letter to the Romans to welcome and honor this beautiful woman who served as a deaconess in her church (Rom. 16:1-2). *Phoebe* was a true wonder woman who had a servant's heart and who used her wealth, talents, and resources for the kingdom of God. It is also worth mentioning these other great women of God: *Eunice* and *Lois*, Timothy's mother and grandmother. They served as two great spiritual role models that instructed him to live a life of faith. The apostle Paul recognized their great accomplishments in raising Timothy in the ways of the Lord (2 Tim. 1:5). *Priscilla, Phoebe, Eunice* and *Lois*, among others, were elevated to Christ's glory. They represented true wonder women who made a difference in the early church: serving, teaching, and ministering with their God-given talents.

Conclusion

Christ not only came to die for the transgressions of mankind, but also to restore women's worth and self-esteem, among other things. In the same manner that Jesus touched and transformed the lives of the women mentioned in this chapter, He can transform us. Today, we no longer have to live in the ashes of sin. In Christ, we are overcomers and have a position of honor. Therefore, we have been elevated to His glory.

His Word promises in the book of Psalms that as we get to know Him and seek a deeper relationship with Him, He will place us in high places (Ps. 91:14-15). Has the enemy taken away your honor and dignity? Has he shattered your identity? Jesus has come to restore your life and lift you up from the ashes of sin to His glory. In Christ you can be made whole.

If you would like to experience deliverance and His glory, I invite you to join me as we say this Prayer.

Prayer for God's Glory

Dear Heavenly Father, I thank You for sending Your only Son, Jesus Christ, to die on the cross for my sins. I thank you for His precious blood that can redeem me from my iniquities. I ask that You please restore my joy, peace, health, family, honor, and wealth; all of which sin and Satan have stripped away from me. Please give me deliverance from all the bondage that sin has placed upon my soul. I pray that I may find my true identity in You and that You may show me Your awesome glory in the midst of my hardships. I ask that I may walk with You in those high places that You have set apart for me. As I continue to pursue a relationship with You, may Your Spirit help me to discover and apply Your truths that will allow me to be that true wonder woman You are seeking. In Jesus' name, I ask. Amen.

Chapter Three: Part 1:
Traits of a True Wonder Woman

A woman's beauty is reflected by her true character.
"A wife of noble character who can find?
She is worth far more than rubies" (Prov. 31:10).

Have you ever seen a beautiful woman on TV or elsewhere and said to yourself, "I wish I could look like her or be able to do the things that she does"? Let's be honest: we have all done that. In our lifetimes, we have admired someone in a good way. Even the most secure woman in the world has a female character whom she looks up to. There are women out there that have caught our attention because of their great accomplishments, abilities, traits, beauty, or sense of style. They have left a trademark or have special characteristics which we are tempted to imitate. I remember when Jennifer Aniston, who played the character of Rachel from the 90s TV show *Friends,* caused a great sensation because of her special haircut. People called it "the Rachel look." It was the hairdo of that decade, and every woman was copying her hairstyle, including me.

Like I said, we have the tendency to admire other women, especially those who have made a difference in our world, and copy their style. When I was a child, I admired my pastor's wife. She was an inspiration to my life and modeled godly living. She was caring, smart, beautiful, poised, elegant, and gifted. She traveled doing missionary work in different countries, utilizing all of her God-given talents. Her heart's desire was to make a difference in other people's lives. I told myself that when I grew up, I'd be like her. Likewise, we esteem our mothers for their self-sacrificing and unconditional love. We also look up to women that fight for good causes and those who are fighting for our freedom.

Whether we are famous or not, we ought to keep in mind that in some ways, we are all role models to other women because we are observed by the people around us. I am such in the eyes of my daughters, family, friends, and those who surround me. For that reason, I know that I must do my best to speak, act, and live in a manner that is pleasing to God so that others want to imitate His goodness in me. The apostle Paul advises us in the book of Romans as to how we ought to live our lives in the midst of people. He says, "...Be careful to do what is right in the eyes of everyone" (Rom. 12:17). Bobby Houston, who is a renowned conference speaker and a pastor's wife from the Hillsong Church in Australia, declares that women have the power to be an influence in other women's lives. I love the way that she expresses herself concerning how our positive way of living becomes an ultimate compliment in her book, *I'll Have What She's Having*. This is what she says:

"Could it be the ultimate compliment? Could it be the most rewarding compliment a person could receive? That someone would observe your world, your lifestyle, your attitude, your sense of purpose, resolve and conviction, then desire the same in their own life. I personally believe it is the ultimate compliment and also a mandate that belongs to every Christian woman, young or mature, regardless of whether she is actual leadership or not."[16]

If we are urged to model devout and holy lives, why is it so difficult for some women to become the true wonder women that God intended them to be and capture all the right characteristics of strength and humility? Unfortunately, keeping up a godly standard of living has proven to be quite the challenge in today's culture. There are good women out there who exemplify righteous living that we can imitate. However, we are also bombarded by many different worldly philosophies and erroneous role models who demonstrate all the wrong traits. We are influenced by the media, celebrities on T.V., or by people around us who do not believe in God and have low moral standards. We are constantly facing temptations that hit us from all sides. The world's message to us is, "If you want to fit in, you must give in."

In these modern times, we dwell within a culture that suffers from spiritual and moral decadence. The world promotes women's exploitation through pornography. Adultery, fornication, self-indulgence, illicit sex, violence, and all kinds of sinful lust are the norm in our culture. Sadly, the values of this country have been twisted over time. What was once good is now considered bad, and what was once bad is now accepted as something good. We are constantly assaulted by worldly powers that try to cloud our godly beliefs and Christian character. However, God already knew from the beginning that we would be facing these types of attacks, so He has given us plenty of instructions in His Word that we may know how to tackle today's problems. He has also left us example stories of people who have faced the same challenges that we do now and who have overcome through His power.

One particular story that I will be focusing is the story of the Ephesians. In the book of Ephesians, the apostle Paul makes a powerful prayer, as a petition for deliverance, unto the Christians in Ephesus. They were struggling with spiritual and moral issues in their city, which promoted an unholy atmosphere, all sorts of lustful temptations, and the worshiping of pagan gods. In this chapter, we will explore Paul's prayer. There are several characteristics of his prayer that we can apply to our Christian walk. We will also briefly study the armor of God as a spiritual tool that can equip us for spiritual warfare. It is the Lord's desire that we pursue biblical truths and traits that will lead us to discover and live as His true wonder women. If we seek to acquire them, we will be able to find and release our God-given powers, which will empower us for victorious living during these hard times.

History of the City of Ephesus

Let me share some background history of the city of Ephesus so that we can better understand the trials and temptations that the early Christians faced in this city. *The Baker Encyclopedia of the Bible* describes the riches of Ephesus and its spiritual condition as follows:

"Ephesus was a wealthy city. The multi-storied residences of its upper-middle-class society rested on the north terraces of Mt Koressos. Some homes had mosaic floors and marble walls. Two were found with heated bathrooms. Many had running water. The moral status of the city can be partially ascertained from a centrally located house of prostitution and gambling tables; fertility motifs are evident in the exaggerated sexual features of the Diana statues."[17]

This city was financially prosperous. Its citizens, for the most part, were well-off and able to enjoy the pleasures of many comfortable amenities. However, in the midst of material success, there was also plenty of perversion: bars, brothels, and gaming establishments. The moral and spiritual condition of the city was in ruins. The apostle Paul prayed that the Lord would strengthen Christ's followers in this perverted city that housed heavy demonic influence. David Seal, in the *Lexham Bible Dictionary*, writes, "Ephesus was known as a place of demonic activity…Because of the popularity of magic in Ephesus, the phrase 'Ephesian writings' was used to describe any documents that contained magic formulas and spells." [18]

A False Wonder Woman

Today, we are faced with wrongful role models that can tempt us to stray away from our godly beliefs, and the Christians of Ephesus had the same encounters. Among many gods that were worshiped in the city of Ephesus, there was one in particular that was respected as a super goddess and a role model. The Romans called her Diana, goddess of fertility. Back then, her temple, the temple of Artemis, was considered to be one of the Seven Wonders of the World because it had a capacity to sit more than twenty-four thousand people. In that place, infamous cults practiced their witchcraft. This temple is mentioned in Acts 19:35.

Several years ago, I had the privilege of visiting the National Archaeological Museum of Naples in Italy. It exhibited a statue of the goddess Diana, also known as the Artemis, from Ephesus. I was expecting to see a statue of a beautiful woman, but instead I saw, to my surprise, an unattractive statue with many breasts on her upper torso. Scholars believe that these breasts represented eggs, private parts of male animals, and other mystical symbols. To the Ephesians, Diana reflected a powerful deity who had the ability to lure women to lust for men and vice versa. The worship expected to be rendered to her had a dominant influence on the people of Ephesus and led them to do wickedness.

The Ephesians also believed that Diana had the power to produce great fertility in the land and could cause their fields a plentiful harvest; as a result, they would be enriched. But in order for them to get the results they wanted, they had to bring certain sacrifices into her temple. Such horrendous sacrifices involved orgies among her priests and priestesses, prostitution, and sacrifices of animals and children. Chris Church, in *The Holman Illustrated Bible Dictionary,* explains the customs performed to Diana the goddess of fertility. He writes:

> "Fertility cults attribute the fertility of the cropland and herds to the sexual relations of the divine couple. Sacral sexual intercourse by priests and priestesses or

by cult prostitutes was an act of worship intended to emulate the gods and share in their powers of procreation or else an act of imitative magic by which the gods were compelled to preserve the earth's fertility (1 Kings 14:23–24; 15:12; Hos. 4:14). Transvestism (prohibited in Deut. 22:5) may have been part of a fertility rite like that practiced by the Hittites. Sacrifices of produce, livestock, and even children (2 Kings 17:31; 23:10) represented giving the god what was most precious in life in an attempt to restore order to the cosmos and ensure fertility."[19]

Diana typified a goddess who had the power to give prosperity to those who worshipped her through such wicked deeds as are mentioned above. However, she was not a good model for the Christians of Ephesus to follow in order to live a holy life.

Traits of a True Wonder Woman

Christ-followers were exposed to the city's environment and its moral contamination on a daily basis. The apostle Paul knew that its pressures were overwhelming and that they, in their own human strength, could not withstand the power of darkness that overshadowed their daily communion with God. He then made this powerful prayer: "I pray that out of His **glorious riches He** may **strengthen** you with **power** through **His Spirit** in your **inner being**" [Bold letters added] (Eph. 3:16). There are powerful traits highlighted within Paul's prayer. We will look at these special traits and others that can empower our Christian walk. Such traits can distinguish us as His true wonder women.

Inner Beauty Emanating from God's Glory

What is glory and why do people strive for it? *The Encarta Dictionary* defines glory as an astounding beauty or beauty that inspires feelings of wonder or joy. To have such glory is to have a beauty that stands out. Every woman on this planet deep inside her heart would like to hear someone say about her, "Have you seen that woman? She is amazingly beautiful. It's a pleasure to look at her. She has an outstanding beauty!" It is wonderful to be able to possess this trait called glory that makes you shine wherever you go. In today's society, sadly, the outward appearance has become the number one emphasis in our pop-culture, and people strive to do anything to boost their physical beauty: overspending on beauty products, and enduring cosmetic plastic surgeries and excruciating weight-loss programs. I believe that exercising, eating a healthy diet, and applying some beauty products are all good and recommended to live and look healthy, but when we obsess in the physical exterior in order to obtain glory and beauty, we will suffer some harsh consequences.

The world has a distorted view of what true beauty really is. The pressure of today's beliefs about how women ought to look has devastated our health physically, emotionally, psychologically, and spiritually. As a teenager, I was always a very thin girl. When I got married, I joined my husband in evangelistic ministry. We traveled extensively, and this made it difficult for me to sit down and plan healthy meals. We ate out a lot, and as a result, I gained some weight. Those extra pounds made me the talk of the town. There were times that people were very cruel to me by making harsh comments about my weight. One day, after singing live on a Christian TV program, I immediately got a phone call at the TV station from a so-called friend. I was expecting to hear her say, "Hey, your song was a blessing," but instead, the first thing that came out of her mouth was, "Evie, you look fat as a cow and you look horrible on TV. You need to lose weight if you want to sing on a platform again. People do not like to see fat performers on stage; they look gross." Right there and then, those harsh words made a wound in my heart. It took me some time to realize that it was Satan speaking to me. He utilized a woman who unfortunately lacked wisdom and prudence to tear my spirit down.

The harassment I received back then concerning my weight produced a numerous amount of insecurities in me. The negative words about my looks began to sink into my head. As a young woman, I began to believe that because I was overweight, I wasn't pretty or important enough to be accepted by God or by people. Due to this erroneous idea that Satan planted in my head, I began to develop a poor body image which led me to an eating disorder called bulimia. That disease kept me in spiritual, emotional, and physical bondage, and it almost took my life. Then one day, I surrendered it all to the Lord. He set me free and saved me from certain death. Like any woman in her late 40's, I struggle with some menopausal weight; however, I'm okay with my inner self because I have discovered that God loves me no matter how I look. I know that I have to care for my body, but I have also learned to keep my soul and spirit dwelling in Him for inner peace, assurance, and acceptance.

Because of our busy lives, there are times when we let ourselves go. In those times, we must find the courage to pick ourselves up and find motivation in God to beautify our whole being. Taking care of our physical appearance is important, but only to a certain extent. Beauty products and makeup can help us enhance our pretty features; but when we focus too much on beautifying the external look and neglect to beautify our internal soul, we are missing the mark. We must take into consideration that *real beauty* comes from the *Glory of God.*

The Greek word for *Glory* is *Doxa,* which means the quality of splendid, remarkable appearance—splendor.[20] *Doxa* is a type of glory that is a magnificent, marvelous, and amazing light. God's *doxa* produces a stunning demeanor that causes one to shine. This kind of glory comes exclusively from heaven and is produced solely by the presence of the Lord. Women in the city of Ephesus concentrated primarily on their outward appearance and neglected to seek inner glory. In the midst of a city filled with pride and outward physical vanities, the apostle Paul prayed that his friends from Ephesus would be filled with God's Glory (*doxa*) in order that they would be light in a dark world.

When we are overtaken by and imparted with His glory, His splendor beautifies our souls. As our spirits are being renewed by His amazing presence and light, His Spirit helps us to develop godly traits; therefore, we are able to shine in the darkness and overcome the forces of this world. Although we might be peer pressured to stress solely about our exterior beauty, let us remember that a true wonder woman's genuine beauty is a reflection of the Glory of God that dwells within her. Fill yourself with His *doxa,* which is the *beauty of God.* Allow His glory to be another trait that you are pursuing in order to receive inner spiritual growth. If you permit His majestic splendor to embrace your whole being, you will experience a difference in the way you feel about yourself, and it won't matter to you what people think or say about your looks. When you are filled with His Glory, people may even stop you, and recognize something different about you, they will compliment you. You see, His splendid Glory makes us beautiful. It outweighs our physical flaws because our glorious Lord lives inside of us. His magnificent light shines through us from the inside out. We learn from the Bible that we are His light: "For you were once darkness, but now you are light in the Lord. Live as children of light" (Eph. 5:8).

A dear sister from church gave me a compliment not too long ago. She said, "Pastor Evie, you always look so beautiful, even at the times that I have seen you wearing no makeup and dressed up in jeans and a t-shirt. You still look lovely, and you always look young." She then asked the following questions: "How do you do it? Do you use any particular beauty cream? Is it expensive?" and, "How can I get it?" I replied, "Thank you, Sister, I appreciate the nice compliment. But it is really His *doxa* and grace that covers me and makes me feel and look beautiful." The grace and glory of the Lord can make any woman look and feel awesome, whether she is a teenager or in her 20s, 30s, 40s, 50s or older. I have also learned some wonderful beauty tips that have kept me looking my best. I would like to share them with you. If you would like to add them to your beauty regimen, I encourage you to do the following:

A. Unclog Your Spiritual Pores

For a fresher and younger look, here's my first beauty tip: unclog your spiritual pores. Some of us suffer from blackheads in the area of the nose. They are not too attractive. In order to unclog them, we can use over-the-counter medicine that treats clogged up pores. When you clean the residue of makeup from your face and treat the pores, your face looks more radiant, and you feel so much better. In the same way, the pores of our hearts can get spiritually clogged up with fears and worries. As you get on your knees to pray, release all your worries to the Lord. The Psalmist advises us to "Cast your cares on the Lord and He will sustain you;..." (Ps. 55:22).

When we try to carry our own burdens, the weight of those afflictions can bring our spirits down, causing our spiritual pores to clog up. God wants you to surrender all your troubles to Him and trust that He will see you through. In doing so, you will learn to live a worry-free life. A worry-free life leaves room for us to live longer and feel an overall sense of health and beauty. Excessive worrying can also cause tension and stress in our physical bodies. Stress can lead to different illnesses. It can rob us of sleep, causing mental fogginess, dark circles, and bags under the eyes. For some women, stress can also cause facial acne. The next time you feel overwhelmed and excessively worried; go to God's beauty clinic to get yourself treated. I can assure you that you will come out of there looking ten years younger.

B. Laugh Out Loud!

Release your sense of humor and learn to laugh out loud. King Solomon tells us that laughter is a great remedy for the soul because sadness affects our physical bodies: "A cheerful heart is good medicine, but a crushed spirit dries up the bones" (Prov. 17:22). It is believed that it takes more muscles to frown than to smile. Someone told me that frowning can cause more wrinkles than smiling. So let us smile more and laugh out loud, for laughter, along with God's joy and glory in us, can make the soul joyful and beautiful.

C. Don't Leave the House without Putting on Your DOXA Beauty Cream

I try to remind myself daily to put on my special *doxa* beauty cream. It is free, and it's an exclusive beauty cream not found in the department stores. The Lord wants to fill you with His special glory inwardly and outwardly. His Glory beautifies our hearts, minds, and bodies. It sets us apart to look different and radiant. A true wonder woman is beautiful because she is filled with Christ's beauty. Wherever you and I go, His splendor goes with us, and since we are representing Him here on earth, His Glory makes us look attractive and young. The Psalmist says that in order to find the fountain of youth and life, we must get a hold of God: "For with You is the fountain of life..." (Ps. 36:9).

Once more, I encourage you to release any feelings of insecurity that might be hindering the glory of God from shining within you. He would like to honor you as His shining star. The Psalmist also tells us that as we, as His vessels, glorify Him with our lives; He will exalt us and bring honor to us (Ps. 89:17). Let His *doxa* beautify you, and allow Him to light your way in a world filled with darkness. Remember: although it is important to take care of our outward appearance, our main focus as God's true wonder women should be to enhance the beauty of our souls by seeking His glory.

Heavenly Riches

Shaina once knew the Lord, but backslid. She lived among certain wealthy people who influenced her to make big money, but not in a good way. Their ways of producing it were illegal, and it was dirty money. Her main focus was to make herself rich. She obtained some wealth, and was proud of her huge bank account. One day she lost it all, and in despair she realized that not only was she monetarily bankrupt, but she was also spiritually in ruins. When she found her Savior Jesus Christ again, her life was restored, and she was equipped with a new heart and a new mind. She became enriched with His wisdom for making money with integrity and managing her finances. The Lord multiplied her blessings, and all that she had lost was regained two-fold. But more importantly, her life was enriched with Christ's joy.

The riches of this world are temporary, but His wealth is everlasting and eternal. The Christians from Ephesus were living in a city that was rich in material things but was short of godly reserves. The apostle Paul knew that as humans they lacked strength to overcome not only the sexual temptations but also the temptation to pursue false riches in an ungodly manner. He prayed that they would be filled with God's treasures and with an abundant wealth of divine grace that would sustain them. Are you in need of His heavenly riches? The Lord is wealthy in wisdom, understanding, grace, and so much more. The material possessions of this world do not exceed His resources, nor are they as valuable as what He has to offer. His heavenly bank account is always full, and He wants to share his immense riches with us. His grace, mercies, and blessings flow constantly toward his children. The Bible tells us that if we seek the spiritual riches of God, He will bless us (3 Jn. 1:2).

God wants to bless you richly in all things that pertain to your life, because He loves you. We are encouraged to fix our eyes on God instead of our earthly wealth because worldly possessions are temporary (1 Tim. 6:17). A true wonder woman will live a prosperous life and will never go spiritually broke pursuing His glorious riches. She knows that in finding such heavenly treasure, she obtains an abundance of grace, strength, wisdom, and power.

Supernatural Strength

As the Christians from Ephesus struggled to keep up holy living and maintain their spiritual and moral values, the apostle Paul prayed that they would be strengthened. He knew that they could not withstand their trials, the evil influences around them, and their own carnal desires in their own natural strength because the flesh is weak. They needed their hearts and spirits to be strong, and in order to achieve that, they needed to be equipped with a supernatural strength. How do we obtain such strength? This supernatural strength is administered solely by the Holy Spirit. We are encouraged to seek and acquire this supernatural strength as a character trait, for it surpasses all human abilities and can empower us to overcome the harsh challenges we face daily in the areas of ministry, work, parenting, and marriage. A supernatural strength is needed when we have to endure bad relationships, abuse, spiritual attacks, and temptations. It also helps us to not to give in to our carnal desires.

    I would like to share the case of a woman who had to learn the hard way how to depend on God for that supernatural strength in order to overcome her carnal desires. This is Victoria's story. This is another woman I encountered in my years of pastoral ministry, and I feel that her testimony can be relevant and a blessing to someone who might be walking in her shoes. Victoria had a lovely and charming personality, but underneath, she had a weak spot. She had uncontrollable sexual urges. Shortly after her second divorce, she began to feel lonely and vulnerable. Her desire to be with a man grew strong. I ministered to her and encouraged her to primarily focus on allowing God to restore her inner being before engaging in another relationship.

    As she continued attending church and seeking the Lord, the enemy placed, right in the middle of her path, a wolf dressed in sheep's clothing who pretended to be a Christian. He took notice of Victoria and began to court her. I immediately detected that this man's objectives toward her were not genuine. His intention was to use her in order to satisfy his own sexual cravings. I warned her to stay away from him, but her longing for a man was too strong. She said to me, "Don't worry, Pastor Evie, I can handle myself; I will not fall into temptation." Soon after, she drifted from the Lord and fell into a sinful affair with this man. As a result, she got pregnant. During her pregnancy, she experienced complications that caused her to lose the baby and almost her own life. While she lay on the operating table facing death, she called upon the Lord and repented from her sin. Her Heavenly Father spared her because He loved her and also had a divine purpose for her life.

Victoria re-committed herself to the Lord and surrendered her all to Him. She then completely understood that she needed to fully depend on the Lord's supernatural strength daily, in order to control her carnal desires and continue living a godly, pure life. Victoria abandoned that sinful relationship and decided to pursue her God-given calling. She enrolled in bible school and became a strong Christian, embracing the Holy Spirit for strength, wisdom, guidance, and power over the enemy, her own flesh, and the temptations of the world. She is now doing missionary work, reaching the lost and helping others who were once in her shoes. A true wonder woman can be an overcomer when she learns to completely depend on and embrace God's supernatural strength.

I love watching superhero movies. In recent years, film companies have featured favorite characters such as Superman, Captain America, the Hulk, Thor, and others. What do all of these superheroes have in common? They are all fitted with a supernatural strength. However, this strength has been given to them by a higher source. Even the fictional comic book character Wonder Woman received her powers from the gods of Greek mythology. When the apostle Paul mentioned in his prayer, the words *He may,* he is acknowledging that we can obtain supernatural powers and become true wonder women not from other means or sources, but from *God alone.*

Who is this God who has the power to strengthen us to overcome any obstacle and become a superhero in our own movie called Life? The prophet Isaiah declares in the bible that God is the giver of life and creator of the universe, of earth, and of all living things. His power is awesome and mighty. He's able to defeat the greatest of giants and convert the impossible to possible. The prophet Isaiah tells us of God's power and His willingness to empower us when we are weak. He says,

> "Have you not known? Have you not heard? The LORD is the everlasting God, the Creator of the ends of the earth. He does not faint or grow weary; his understanding is unsearchable. He gives power to the faint, and to him who has no might he increases strength. Even youths shall faint and be weary, and young men shall fall exhausted; but they who wait for the LORD shall renew their strength; they shall mount up with wings like eagles; they shall run and not be weary; they shall walk and not faint" (Isa. 40:28-31).

We are made with a human nature that is weak. Because of it, we are not on our own able to withstand the spiritual storms of this world. That is why we must stay connected to our Heavenly Father. When Jesus lived on earth, He set the perfect example of how a hero obtains his strength. His source of strength was God the Father, who empowered Him to be strong through the power of *the Holy Spi*rit (Lk. 4:1). A true wonder woman's character is strengthened and shaped by God, her Creator. As godly women, we must make the Lord our only source of strength.

Supernatural Power

Another key word in the apostle Paul's prayer for the Christians in Ephesus is the word *power*. The Greek words for power *are dynamei*, which means *to be able and dynamis* to excersice power.[21] This power is a supernatural power that is given by the Holy Spirit. His special power enables us to triumphantly achieve our God-given purpose in life. We can apply this kind of power in all the areas of our lives, especially when facing trials and attacks from the enemy. The apostle Paul desired that the Lord would also equip the Christians with this supernatural power so that they could defeat their spiritual enemy who strived to attack them often through many dangers and spiritual battles. Satan will try to destroy us in any way possible. Therefore, we must be vigilant and filled with the power of the Holy Spirit at all times because we do not know when the devil will show up to strike us down (1 Pet. 5:8).

Allow me to share this story of Juanita, a courageous woman I met many years ago who was filled with God's supernatural power. She shared with me her powerful testimony of how one frightful day she experienced the Lord's supernatural power in her, giving her victory to overcome fear and the enemy in the midst of an assault. While visiting her native country, one afternoon, as she and her husband were traveling by car on rustic roads to visit her mother, they were stopped by two gunmen, accustomed to rob tourists passing by. The gunmen told them to come out. As she and her husband got out of the car, she took her Bible and held it tight. The gunmen asked for her purse, wallet, and the book she had in her hands. She surrendered the purse and wallet, but Juanita did not want to give up the Bible. The gunmen snatched it from her hand and threw it on the ground, mocking her and threatening to kill them both.

Juanita began to pray within her spirit for deliverance. All of a sudden, the Holy Spirit gave her the power and boldness to rebuke the gunmen. She looked straight into their eyes and, as they were pointing the gun at her, she boldly exclaimed, "Satan, I come against you in the name of Jesus. The Word of God assures me in (Isa. 54:17) that 'No weapon formed against me shall prosper'. I command you to leave this very moment in Jesus' name and give me back what belongs to me!" As soon as she finished speaking, the gunmen trembled with fear. They dropped the purse and wallet from their hands and ran off. They were frightened, as if they saw a ghost. She and her husband then went on their way, praising the Lord for his divine power and protection.

What caused the men to tremble with fear? What prompted Juanita to fearlessly face them head on? Juanita serves as a good example of how a true wonder woman ought to act in the face of her enemy's threats. She carries the traits of a woman who is spiritually equipped in the midst of adversity. In order to answer the questions above, let us further analyze how this wonder woman handled the situation. When Juanita found herself in danger, she called on God. We have our own heavenly 911 emergency number that we can dial when we are facing danger. King David surely knew how to use it. Whenever he was threatened by the enemy, he simply dialed "Help me God!" You can find this number in the white pages of the book of Psalms, which says, "This poor man called, and the Lord heard him; he saved him out of all his troubles" (Ps. 34:6).

Whenever you find yourself in danger, be assured that God will always come to your rescue when you pray to Him. Our prayers activate the hand of God to move in our direction for favor and protection. I am sure that the gunmen were frightened not by Juanita but by her bodyguard. God must have opened their eyes to see who was standing in front of her. I imagine this invisible protector as very tall, well-equipped for battle, and intimidating enough to scare away those bullies. It is reassuring to know that the Lord assigns us our own personal spiritual body guard to shield us. When the enemy comes around, this supernatural warrior fights courageously and victoriously against him. No one messes with God's children. King David confirms this in the book of Psalms. He tells of the heavenly, invisible warrior who protects the Lord's people: "The angel of the Lord encamps around those who fear him, and he delivers them" (Ps.34:7).

In a moment of crisis, Juanita experienced a *dynamis* of the Holy Spirit which gave her success over the gunmen. Dynamis is so powerful that it has the capability of exploding as a detonated bomb. It is a supernatural power that surpasses our natural human strength. This type of power weakens and defeats our spiritual enemy. Our source of power is exclusively drawn from God's Spirit. He gives us the boldness to stand up to and conquer our adversary and also overcome the hardships of life. In order to obtain a *dynamis* power that is produced by the Holy Spirit, we must first receive authority from a higher source.

The Bible tells us that Jesus Christ gives us the authority and power to crush and dismantle not some but *all* of Satan's powers. He says, "I have given you authority to trample on snakes and scorpions and to overcome *all* the power of the enemy; nothing will harm you" (Lk. 10:19). Be assured that as you seek the Holy Spirit, you will be empowered with his special *dynamis*. No devil or demonic force can defeat a woman filled with His great and mighty power. A true wonder woman is characterized by Christ's power in her. She distinctively walks and talks with a confidence that is established and rooted in the Holy Spirit. Let us strive to acquire this unique trait that will enable us to live as conquerors in all the areas of our lives, and may we not forget that we are great victors in Christ Jesus, as stated in (Rom.8:37).

Holy Spirit

Before Jesus ascended to heaven, He promised his disciples that they were not going to be left alone to fend for themselves. They were to receive a special gift from heaven (Acts 1:4). This gift was the *Holy Spirit*. Who is the Holy Spirit? He is the third person of the Trinity (Mt. 3:16). Jesus said, "But the Comforter (Counselor, Helper, Intercessor, Advocate, Strengthener, Stand by), the Holy Spirit, Whom the father will send in My name (in My place, to represent Me and act on My behalf). He will teach you all things" (Jn. 14:26). The Greek word for *helper* is *paraklētos* which means "summoned, called to one's side, esp. called to one's aid."[22] The Holy Spirit is our *parakletos*. He helps us in all our circumstances. He is a magnificent and all-powerful person who imparts to us the power of Christ (Acts 1:8; Matt.28:18).Jesus told his disciples that they would receive the power of the Holy Spirit in order to witness about Him to all Jerusalem and all the world (Acts 1:8). It was not an easy task because their world was influenced by the evil forces of Satan, and whoever dared to speak about Jesus could run the risk of getting killed. The early church suffered persecution because of the name of Christ. The disciples needed the help of the Holy Spirit to carry out the Lord's command to spread the gospel.

Today, we are facing times when our nation and the world no longer want to accept the name of God or Christ's teachings in our schools, homes, families, businesses, and public places. The world embraces ungodly standards, and anyone who opposes them runs the risk of being mocked; some have been thrown in jail, and others have been executed and persecuted. In a city, school, home, and country where God is absent, there will be an abundance of spiritual darkness.

Now more than ever, we are in need of the Holy Spirit to give us boldness to go forth and speak of His marvelous kingdom. The apostle Paul knew that if the Christians of Ephesus were going to be overcomers in the midst of their city, they would have to seek the Holy Spirit. Life's challenges, trials, and spiritual dark forces can be overwhelming to our human nature, but, through the Holy Spirit in us, we are able to rise above. The Holy Spirit will provide the necessary comfort, guidance, inspiration, conviction, deliverance, transformation, peace, and power to triumph over all our hardships and over all the evil influences in our world. The following are some tools available through the Holy Spirit.

The Gifts and the Fruit of the Spirit

The gifts of the Spirit are given to the believer by the Holy Spirit for the purpose of edifying one another. They are: wisdom, knowledge, faith, healing, miracles, prophecy, discernment of spirits, speaking in different kinds of tongues, and interpretation of tongues **(1 Cor.12:8-10)**. We are encouraged to seek and utilize the gifts of the Spirit, but can we be effective in our ministries and in our Christian walk without the fruit of the Spirit?

The following are three examples of women who possess certain gifts of the Spirit but fall short by failing to implement the fruit of the Spirit. The stories illustrate the importance of recognizing and implementing not only our personal spiritual gifts, but also the qualities of the spiritual fruit that correspond to them. Leila is a talented woman. She carries great gifts of the Spirit, such as the gifts of wisdom, knowledge, and prophecy. She loves to counsel people and serve the needy. She has many admirable traits. However, when things do not go her way, she loses her temper and tells people off without mercy. Lacy is another sweet woman. She too is gifted with the gifts of the Spirit and other talents. She frequently complains that no one understands her gifts or that the women of the church often avoid her. One night, at a woman's gathering, Lacy began to pray for a young woman. According to Lacy, she was utilizing her gift of knowledge in releasing this woman's most intimate secrets out loud for everyone to hear. The young woman was embarrassed, and this caused conflict between them. Visitors who attended that night were turned off and never returned to church.

Tabitha is also a very exceptional and skilled person with a lot of creativity and certain gifts of the Spirit. She wonders why the women of the church do not befriend her. Unfortunately, she has some undesirable traits. She is known as a woman who is judgmental, prideful, and untruthful. She never owns up to her mistakes and craves titles and positions in the church. Because of this, she does not care whose toes she steps on in order to get her way. She also possesses a self-centered spirit that wants attention at any cost.

As we observe these three Christian women, we notice that they own talents and gifts of the Spirit and love to serve in church, but they lack a Christ-like character. As a result, people are not moved by their gifts and talents. Let's be honest: Christians are not perfect. We are simply human beings who have struggles like everyone else. However, as Christ's followers, we are urged by Jesus to die to our sinful nature and corrupt attitudes on a daily basis (Gal.5:24). God is looking for a woman through whom He may display His awesome love and power for the purpose of reaching out to all those people who are in need of His touch.

How can we each become that true wonder woman the Lord is searching for? We are encouraged through God's Word to exemplify a life filled with the fruit of the Spirit. When Jesus lived on earth, the fruit of the Spirit abounded in Him, and through the Holy Spirit in Him, the gifts of the Spirit were also manifested. He performed miracles, signs, and wonders, and healed and restored hurting people with God's power, love, compassion, and humility. I agree with Alex Nes in his book, The Holy Spirit-Volume Two. He says, "Only out of a life abounding with the fruit of the Sprit should the gifts be manifested."[23] What is the fruit of the Spirit? "The Greek word for *fruit* is *karpos*, which is in singular form. It is called the *fruit* and not the *fruits* because it is a nine-fold fruit as one cluster"[24]

As the Holy Spirit uses us with His spiritual gifts, we are encouraged to display a Christ-like character and demonstrate the fruit of the Spirit: love, joy, peace, forbearance, kindness, goodness, faithfulness, gentleness, and self-control

(Gal. 5:22-23). The fruit of the Spirit helps the believer to build a Christ-like character. In order to be Christian women who are effective in ministering to others, we must allow ourselves to be formed and molded into the character of Christ and embrace the fruit of the Spirit. Our spiritual gifts have to match the fruit of the Spirit in us. They go hand in hand.

If we minister to people, we ought to do so with a character of integrity, compassion, humility, and love. If we focus only on ministering to others with our gifts without demonstrating a Christ-like attitude, then our ministry and gifts will not be able to impact and make a difference in people's lives. We can cultivate godly traits by building a Christ-like character and committing whole-heartedly to a relationship with Christ. Character and the fruit of the Spirit are connected. As we grow in Him, we will be able to produce spiritual fruit and will develop characteristics that are worthy to be imitated. There are many good women in the world, but God's true wonder woman stands out and is sought after for her godly traits.

When the apostle Paul prayed that the Holy Spirit would strengthen the inner being of the Christians of Ephesus, he was praying for their hearts to be stronger. The inner being has to do with the heart. The heart is one of the main internal organs of a human body. Without a heart, it is impossible to live. Every heartbeat produces life. The heart may be small, but its functions are vital. There are two important things we must do in order to build a Godly heart: we must guard our hearts from temptations, and we must cultivate a worthy heart.

A. Guard Your Heart

Although the heart is a small organ, some of the greatest desires have been born from it. However, the most perverted masterplans have also been birth from the heart. Solomon advises us of how crucial it is to guard our hearts. Such a tiny organ has the power to do either great good or extreme harm. He implies that above all other organs in our bodies and beyond all else, we must safeguard our hearts because thoughts, emotions, feelings, desires and our actions are driven from it (Prov. 4:23). What we think, what we say, and how we act come either from a sinful nature or a godly one embedded within the core of our hearts.

The Holy Spirit's main desire is to live inside of us. As He dwells within our being, He begins to strengthen and empower us to be strong and resilient to the temptations and struggles of sin that fight us daily, but we must do our part as well. We must keep our hearts by not giving in to temptations and sinful desires. The Holy Spirit works with us to help guard our hearts from the evil that comes from our sinful nature and also the evil that comes from the world. As we seek Him in prayer on an everyday basis, our inner self becomes transformed, and then we are able to work on developing a heart that God approves of.

B. Cultivate a Worthy Heart

Now, how can we cultivate a worthy heart, one with which the Lord would be pleased? The apostle Peter shares a formula by which we can obtain a kind of heart that pleases God, and it is developing a gentle and quiet spirit within us (1

Pet. 3:4). My observation of what the apostle Peter is saying is that having a gentle and quiet spirit means to have a heart that is meek and humble. Moses was considered to be the meekest and most humble person in all the land (Num. 12:3). He dealt with many difficult people who were always complaining and grumbling. However, Moses showed patience and meekness in those difficult times. The Lord was pleased with his gentle and quiet heart. A woman with a gentle and quiet heart is slow to speak and quick to listen. She is meek and humble. When someone says something offensive and hurtful, her quiet heart does not reply with hostility; rather, it forgives and releases the hurt to the Lord.

The Bible tells us we should listen before we speak, instead of rushing to blurt out our opinions or frustrations in anger (Jm.1:19-20). Quick answers generated by our negative emotions do not lead to the righteousness that God desires for us. A woman with a gentle and quiet heart is of great value to the Lord. Of course, having a worthy heart does not happen overnight. It takes time to learn how to guard our hearts correctly, it takes practice in every situation of life to make the right choices, and it takes teamwork with the Holy Spirit to build these characteristics. As you work on these things in the power of the Holy Spirit, you will soon notice the change in your heart!

As the apostle Paul prayed that his friends' hearts would be strengthened and that they would cultivate godly characteristics, it is my prayer that we too obtain such worthy traits that will please God and lead us to live peaceful lives. In the second part of this chapter, we will continue to explore more powerful traits and tools, such as the armor of God, which can enable a true wonder woman to find and release her God-given powers and become a spiritual warrior.

Chapter Three: Part 2:

A great soldier is always equipped and ready for battle.

Spiritual Warrior

Ann, along with her husband, was called by God to open up a mission in Mexico. When she arrived there, she was deliberately attacked by an evil spirit. One night at around ten thirty, while her husband was walking the dog, she was alone in her room and was getting ready to read her Bible and pray. At that moment, she felt a presence standing behind her. All of a sudden, it pushed her violently. She landed face down, and her knee hit the metal of the bed frame. When she tried to stand up, she was unable to do so. Her knee had come out of its joint socket. In agony, she crawled and managed to get into bed. This true wonder woman was a spiritual warrior; her distress did not stop her from fighting her enemy and claiming her victory. As she spent all night in prayer, she told the Lord, "If you healed the sick back then, I know that you can heal me too."

The clock struck at two in the morning when, at the foot of her bed, she saw two hands stretched forward. They were God's hands that grabbed her leg and began to move it gently. Anne testified, "The tears were rolling down my face, as I felt the gentleness of my Master holding my leg. After sometime of aligning it, He put it in place and healed it. As He placed my leg back on the bed, I cried, 'Lord Jesus!' He remained with his hands outstretched for some time and then disappeared." Ann had left her family, friends, and church to pursue her calling in a rural city in Mexico. It was her desire to impact lives by sharing God's Word, her time, her money, and her talents. This made Satan very angry.

When we decide to obey God's calling and set our hearts to make a difference in others, you better believe that we are a target of the devil. He will try at all costs to stop us from moving forward in our walk with Jesus. The apostle Paul tells us that even though we physically live in this world, we will struggle with evil forces in the spiritual realm (Eph. 6:12). It is not my intention to give the devil glory or to make you afraid. My purpose is to bring an awareness of his existence, the spiritual warfare that we constantly confront, and the way we can overcome. There are people and even Christians who believe that Satan does not exist, and that he is just a myth invented for horror movies. I would like to say that he is very real and also God's enemy. He hates us because we are the Lord's creation. Satan wages war against us, God's children, to destroy us.

As God's true wonder women, we are called to seek the traits of a spiritual warrior. A spiritual warrior equips herself completely with the armor of God in order to defeat her spiritual enemy. Briefly, we will explore the pieces of the armor of God and learn how we can utilize them in our everyday lives for victorious living.

The Armor of God

Can a policeman wearing casual, civilian clothes stop traffic? Is he able to apprehend someone who has broken the law without his armament? If he is not wearing his police uniform or if he is not equipped with the right weapons, in the first case, no one would listen to him, and in the second, he would not have much success in catching the criminal. His uniform and weapons empower him and give him authority in order to do his job effectively. While living in this world filled with spiritual darkness, we, as God's true wonder women, need to be always ready and equipped for battle. In the book of Ephesians, the apostle Paul recommends that we use Godly spiritual tools to overcome Satan and his evil forces. Paul says, "Therefore put on the full armor of God, so that when the day of evil comes, you may be able to stand your ground, and after you have done everything, to stand" (Eph. 6:13). A smart soldier is fully armored at all times. However, some Christians walk with no armor on and others carry only half of it. When we are unarmed, we are vulnerable, and if we only carry half of it, we may find ourselves spiritually debilitated. The apostle Paul tells us to clothe our spiritual selves with the *whole* armor. In doing so, we become empowered to courageously stand against the cunning schemes of our adversary. So let's take some time to examine the specific pieces of armor as illustrated in (Eph.6:13-17).

The Belt of Truth. The apostle Paul admonishes us to "Stand firm therefore, having girded your loins with truth." (v.14a, NASB). Why was this piece of armor mentioned first? Paul makes a metaphorical comparison between a Roman soldier's armor and our spiritual armor. Roman soldiers had to fight many difficult and challenging battles. Before they went into battle, they were ordered to be ready and equipped with their entire suit of armor. The first things they specifically put on was a belt around their midriffs. This belt was crucial because it protected and covered the body parts below the waist that were vulnerable, like their thighs and groins. The belt had to be securely fastened around their waists to also support other parts of the armor.

In spiritual terms, this means that we must wrap ourselves in truth. As spiritual warriors, we are to maintain a position of readiness to respond always in truthfulness and with sincerity. What truth are we talking about? The apostle Paul declares that Jesus Christ is the truth and His truth sets us free; it produces true joy, peace, and blessings (Jn. 14:6). It can totally transform our inner-self, our attitudes, behavior, and our way of living; helping us to build Godly traits (Eph. 4:15). This can happen if only we allow His truth to dictate our Christian walk. It is Satan's goal to weaken us in battle. How can he do that? The enemy wins territory over us when we permit our sinful nature to do what it wants to do. Our sinful nature wants to speak lies, steal, cheat, and do all that is contrary to what the Lord's Word tells us to do. A true wonder woman is strengthened by the belt of truth. It empowers her to walk, talk, and apply the truth of Christ's Word to her everyday life. She no longer is operating under the fruit of the flesh, giving Satan opportunities to win over her, but instead she is walking in God's truth (Eph. 4:27). As a result, she is able to defeat him at the battleground. This piece of armor allows her to successfully fight and overcome the devil.

The Breastplate of Righteousness. The apostle Paul advises us to put "the breastplate of righteousness in place" (v. 14b). Roman soldiers used breastplates as a piece of armor that was made out of iron to protect their chests from sharp weapons or swords. The Greek word for breast plate is *thoraka* meaning "a shield toward our Christian standards. It is also used figuratively in the New Testament to indicate the protective values of certain Christian virtues: '…we must wear faith and love as a breastplate' 1Thessalonians 5:8."[25] We are urged to put on the *thoraka*, or the breast plate of righteousness, in order to protect our faith, our Christian beliefs, and our moral principles.

The Lord requires that we live a life of holiness and righteousness. God's message through His Word tells us to do what is right and honest. Therefore we ought not to lie, steal, cheat, and commit murder. However, in the world we live in, we are also being bombarded by a different kind of message. The world promotes and celebrates messages of unrighteousness. Its agenda is to tear down our Christian beliefs and Godly standards. In a subtle way, we are influenced by their teachings as they promote immorality and witchcraft through the media. We have become desensitized, as we sit in front of our TV and watch movies that promote lying, stealing, cheating, and murder. We are not affected anymore as we watch our favorite female protagonist lie and cheat in order to steal some other woman's husband and at the end of the movie we applaud with contentment in our hearts because our favorite couple ended up together. At that moment, we did not realize that the vows of a marriage that was once said at an altar was violated and broken. I ask myself, "What has happened to us?" We have allowed unrighteous messages to entertain us.

We are also not aware of how much witchcraft is introduced in the shows that we watch. The Bible condemns witchcraft (Rev. 21:8). Today, people acknowledge mediums as professionals with an ability to see the future, and so people celebrate and seek them for their gift. They do not realize that these people are conjuring and are trying to take the place of God by joining forces with Satan. When we have conformed ourselves to watching the unrighteous and immoral messages that are being projected through a lot of these TV programs and movies, we run the danger of being deceived. The Bible warns us to be careful in what we accept to believe and to test every spirit, because not everything that we watch and hear are godly, and they can influence us to lead a life of unrighteousness (1 Jn.4:1). And so, we are encouraged to put on the breastplate of righteousness, in order to shield our hearts and minds from deceiving messages that do not comply with the Word of God and that can lead us astray from our faith. As His true wonder women, we are called to live in righteousness and uphold our Christian standards, even when no one else will. The breastplate of righteousness helps us not to compromise our biblical values.

Feet Fitted. The apostle Paul urges us to get our *feet fitted* with the gospel of peace, meaning that feet, fitted, designates preparedness to fight (v. 15). The Gospel of the Good News gives you solidity and the swiftness to face your enemy face to face. You can stand up to him and nothing will waver or move you when you are in a state of readiness. According to Spence-Jones, in his book, *"The Pulpit Commentary: Ephesians,"* the Roman soldiers used sandals that were built to keep them steady on their feet. This is how they define the fitted feet that the apostle Paul was referring to: "The Roman sandal was furnished with nails that gripped the ground firmly, even when it was sloping or slippery; so the good news of peace keeps us upright and firm."[26] As we start our day, it is important get our spiritual feet fitted by taking the time to pray and meditate in His Word. In doing so, as we deliver Christ's Gospel to others, we are empowered to demolish any demonic attacks without being shaken.

The Shield of Faith. We are told to "Take up the shield of faith, with which you can extinguish all the flaming arrows of the evil one" (v. 16). Another important piece of armor that the Roman soldiers utilized was a shield. The Greek word for *shield* is *thyreos*.[27] Thyreos is the four-cornered long shield which covers the whole man like a door.[28] Roman soldiers used this special shield to protect themselves from flying arrows. Such weapons or arrows were drenched with a flammable substance, in order to burn their victims. Satan will also use his fiery arrows to burn our faith down into ashes and cause us to disbelieve in God's Word.

Doors are meant to protect from the harsh weather and from intruders to come inside your home. In the same manner, a *shield* is designed to protect from dangerous weapons. The apostle Paul encourages us to cover our whole being with the shield of faith as if we were metaphorically covering ourselves with a big door. Getting a hold of such faith in God's Word as a spiritual shield can protect our minds and hearts from the spiritual flaming arrows of doubts, fears, pride, unbelief and any negative thoughts fueled by the enemy. It can also empower us to tear down and extinguish the enemy's armament. We can succeed over our hardships, trials and our adversary, when we guard ourselves with faith in God and in His promises. As His wonder women, it is imperative to put on the shield of faith at all times.

The Helmet of Salvation. The apostle Paul also encourages us to "Take the helmet of salvation." (v. 17). No Roman soldier would fight in combat without this vital piece of armor. It is believed that the helmet was made out of bronze metal to protect the head from dangerous blows coming from swords. What does the helmet of salvation means to us and how can we apply it in our Christian walk? The Greek word for *helmet* is *perikephalaia*…it is the protection of the soul which consists in (the hope of) salvation.[29]

The world tells us that Christ is a myth and that there is no eternal life with Him. This piece of armor serves as a reminder and assurance that in Christ, who is the hope of our salvation, we are saved (Jn. 10:28). We then can continue serving the Lord with confidence, knowing for certain that as we remain faithful to Him, we will someday soon live with Him in eternity. It is also assuring to know that when we are in need of that divine protection, as we take up the helmet of salvation, we can count on Him to see us through during times of battles. The Psalmist declared, "O Sovereign Lord, my strong deliverer, who shields my head in the day of battle" (Ps. 140:7).

The Sword of the Spirit. The apostle Paul admonishes that as spiritual warriors, we ought to take up, "The Sword of the Spirit, which is the Word of God" (Eph. 6:17). The Word of God is a weapon that is "sharper than any double-edged sword" (Heb. 4:12). It cuts deep into the heart, causing conviction and transformation. The Roman soldiers utilized a sword as their main weapon to attack and to defend themselves. During Jesus' forty days of fasting in the desert, He was tempted by Satan (Matt. 4:1-11). He set the example for us on how a Christian ought to fight the devil. Christ as the Son of God used no physical weapons or His great powers to defeat the enemy; instead He utilized Scriptures as a sword. When Jesus was hungry, the devil told him, "If you're the Son of God, turn these stones into bread," but right away Jesus fought back with the Scriptures and said, "It is written, "Man shall not live by bread alone but by every word that comes out of the mouth of God" (vv. 3-4). Each time the devil came around to tempt Jesus, he was beaten in every round. The Word of God was successful as Christ's offense and defense.

What can we learn from Jesus's strategy in combating the enemy? His Word is a powerful sword and tool in our hands. It can tear down the devil, causing a blow straight into his chest. As His true wonder women, we must utilize the Scriptures to fight the devil. Read His Word daily, memorize scriptures and hold His promises close to your heart. It will empower you to become a victor and not his victim.

Conclusion

People are seeking a superhero to look up to. They are looking for someone with desirable traits to imitate. As daughters of God, through His glory in us, we can shine like beacons in the darkness and can make a difference. In the same manner that the early Christians struggled with perversion and wrongful role models in their city, we too share the same challenges in our own modern Ephesus. However, we can be successful in overcoming spiritual attacks, Satan and our own sinful desires if we put on God's armor and seek and apply Godly traits. This will empower us to walk victoriously and will distinguish us as His true wonder women.

Prayer for Godly Traits

Dear Heavenly Father, I thank You for your divine Holy Spirit. I recognize that You are my source of strength. I ask that as I navigate through the sea of life, Your Spirit would equip me with tools that will empower me to overcome all hardships and temptations, and in addition that I may acquire your special godly traits. I ask that my inner being would be enhanced with Your heavenly treasures. Enrich me with wisdom, power and strength as I pursue the fruit of your Spirit and build a Christ-like character. It is my desire that Your light shine in my life, in order that other women may witness Your glory and be inspired to seek Your holy presence. I ask all this in Jesus' name. Amen.

Chapter Four

If God rested on the seventh day, after creating the world; even superheroes are entitled to a holiday.

Beating the Do it All Syndrome

𝒮ilvia wondered why she felt so tired as she woke up to the sound of her alarm clock buzzing loudly at her ear. She then recalled that she had only gotten a few hours of sleep; not enough to give her a good rest. Unsuccessfully, she extended her hand to turn off the buzzer a couple of times, but the alarm clock continued buzzing, relentlessly. It was as if it were telling her, "Hey, get up, it's six o'clock. Duty calls!" Her body is exhausted and unwilling to budge, but this thing called the *To-Do List* is standing right in front of Silvia, wrapping itself around her mind and soul, acting as if it was a Navy lieutenant commanding her to get out of bed. "Okay, okay, I'm up and ready for action," she says to herself. Rubbing her eyes and taking a deep breath, she manages to get up from bed. She looks up to heaven and sends God a telegram saying, "Good morning God, please be with me this day."

Silvia starts off her day with a quick shower. She finishes getting ready and then gently tries to wake up the kids. She then proceeds to make breakfast, prepare lunch boxes and open the kitchen back door so that Rufus, the dog, can go out and do his business. The clock is ticking and time is of the essence. She strives to get everything and everybody ready in order to make it to school and her job on time, which is all before eight thirty. So far everyone is cooperating, except for little Johnny. He's still in bed, no surprise there. Silvia looks at her watch and it's ten minutes after eight. By this time her stress level is increasing and her hormones are going crazy. She starts screaming like a sergeant, "Johnny, you better get out of bed and get down here now or you're going to get it!" Everyone else is getting into the car, but Silvia is still inside the house making sure that the dog has fresh water and food. She then rapidly takes out the meat from the freezer so that it will be unfrozen to cook when she gets back. Furthermore, she puts the last load of dirty laundry in the washer, turns off all the lights and gives her husband a goodbye kiss. Then she drops the kids off at school and finally makes it to work, barely on time. Before she walks through the door, she takes another deep breath and composes herself in order to get her mind ready for work.

As Silvia arrives at her work station, she finds a very long to-do list that was placed on her desk by her boss. He expects her to fulfill most of it by the end of the week. Silvia begins to feel overwhelmed as she thinks to herself, "Is there an end to this To-Do List? Doesn't my boss know that I have a life? I'm going to have to take some of this work and finish it at home." The clock strikes five o'clock, indicating that her first job is over. She anxiously walks out the door and gets in her car. She begins to collect her thoughts and is going over her next To-Do List, which pertains to her second job at *home*, the one for which she isn't paid. As she heads over to pick up the kids from the after school care, she finds herself tackling the rush hour traffic and because of it, she makes it there late. As a result of her tardiness, she is forced to pay a late pickup fee for childcare.

Still dealing with the fact that she has a deadline to meet at work, she tries to make dinner as quickly as possible. Her busy life is infused with the stress of work and home, but her day isn't over just yet. While making dinner, she glances at Timmy's homework to help him solve a math problem. All of a sudden, the phone rings and her husband, who also came home tired from work, is unwinding in front of the TV watching his pre-recorded game. He hollers at her from his throne (a.k.a. reclining leather chair) saying, "Honey, please pick up the phone!" She manages on with one hand stirring the pot as she cooks, the other hand is holding the cell phone, and with her foot, she is able to push the kitchen door open so that the dog can go out again. Does this scenario seem familiar?

Antonia, the leader of her church's women's ministry, is calling Silvia to ask her if she can stop by the church's kitchen on Saturday for a few hours to help make the tamales for Sunday's church Fundraiser. Silvia hesitates for a moment. She's thinking that she has to finish that work project that is due, but can't find the heart to say no, and so she says, "No problem Antonia, you can count on me to be there." After eating dinner and helping the kids finish their homework, she gets them ready to go to the Wednesday family night service held at seven o'clock. Silvia is also a girls' ministry sponsor at her local church. By nine o'clock they rush home. She makes sure that the kids get their baths and tucks them into bed; then she cleans up the kitchen and folds the laundry. Her husband sees her busy and tells her, "Honey, while you're doing your thing, I'll catch up with the late news and then I'll go to bed." She replies back, "Babe, don't wait up for me, because when I'm done with the house chores, I have to spend a couple of hours on my work project that is due soon.

She stays up until midnight working but then she slowly starts to feel exhaustion creep in and decides to give it a rest. Afterwards, she brushes her teeth and slips into her pajamas. By this time, she is completely drained and is very much looking forward to sinking her head into her pillow. As she is pulling the blanket, getting comfortable in her spot, she closes her eyes and gets ready to doze off. All of a sudden, in the midst of the dark room she feels a hand rubbing her leg and hears a sweet voice whispering in her ear. It was not the voice of the Holy Spirit but rather the voice of her husband. He gently and persuasively tells her, "Honey, let's do it, I'm in the mood" and sure enough that's what I call, *working overtime*!

It's overtime work, for a wife who not only has to be a homemaker and a working mom but also has to fulfill her marital duties any time of the night her husband wants it. Sometimes her duties continue throughout the night, caring for sick or otherwise needy children. After learning about a day in Silvia's life, we realize why she is so tired and why she has such a hard time getting up in the morning. Her life is somewhat of a typical working mother, which I can relate to because I've been there and done that and so have many of you who have a busy life and can also be wrapped up in a *Do it All* syndrome. In this chapter, we will define the Do it All syndrome, its effects, and how the Word of God instructs us on how we can we beat it.

I once heard someone say a joke on TV that was not only funny but made a lot of sense. He said, "If a rich man needs his house clean and his laundry done, he hires a *maid*. If he needs food on the table, he hires a *chef*. If he needs someone to watch his kids, he hires a *nanny*. If he is sick and needs home care, he hires a *nurse*. If he needs someone to look over his business accounts, answer his phone calls and pay his bills, he hires an *assistant/receptionist*. If he needs to get things fixed in the house, he hires a *handyman*. However for a man that is monetarily poor and needs all of the above, all he has to do is simply *get married*." Can one woman be and do all that? You better believe she can!

Women can Multitask

God made women with exceptional capabilities. Some say that women can sustain severe pain better than man. Can a man be able to endure the agony of giving birth? Can you picture in your mind your husband being nine months pregnant and enduring labor pains? Would he be able to survive? I don't think so! Birthing a child can cause horrendous and excruciating pains. I think that men would agree with me that it would be a hilarious and uncomfortable scenario for them. That is why they were not designed to give birth and endure such a glorious event. Heaven gave women that task.

Another remarkable aptitude that women possess is the ability to multitask. They can perform many roles all at once. At home when our children are sick, who do they call first? They call for mommy instead of daddy. It is because a mother has a divine warm and healing touch and also has the capacity to play the role of a nurse. We not only take the role of a nurse. We are maids, waitresses, chefs, chauffeurs, sisters, contractors, daughters, lovers, career women, professionals, pastors, ministers, leaders, and the list goes on. Although we wear a lot of hats, I would like to acknowledge those single dads who serve their family and who play both roles of mom and dad. Likewise, we are grateful for the men in this generation that do get involved with the caring of their children, who cook dinners, and who are considerate toward their wives. But there is only so much that they can do or choose to do.

Men and women are both competent at multitasking, however, researchers have found through extensive study and testing that women are able and also are more involved in multitasking than men are when it came to doing house chores and looking after the kids. Having this virtue of multitasking and being able to juggle many roles and tasks is admirable and you can proclaim that it does qualify one to be called a "wonder woman." But having said all that, we can also fall into a dysfunctional pattern which I call the Do it All syndrome.

What is Do it All Syndrome?

The Merriam-Webster dictionary defines the word syndrome as "a disease or disorder that involves a particular group of signs and symptoms." When someone suffers from any kind of syndrome, it indicates that there is a dysfunction or disorder in their lives. In my perspective, a woman who suffers from a Do it All syndrome is a woman who suffers symptoms of perfectionism and obsesses in producing and doing more than she can at any cost. She does not believe or practice delegation. She deeply thinks that she does not need anyone's help. She can go on and on and on trying to get everything done all at once by herself and is completely relying solely on her own strength.

We are encouraged to always strive to do and perform our duties to the best of our abilities in caring for our family, work, careers or ministry, but when we obsess in thinking that we can do it all with our own strength, then our lives will suffer from exhaustion and we can ultimately experience a burnout. Having this kind of mentality can eventually lead us to collapse emotionally, physically, and spiritually.

What Does the Bible Reveal Concerning Doing it All?

The demands of our busy lifestyle can sometimes be overwhelming. Can we accomplish it all in our own power? What does the Word of God tell us? The apostle Paul instructs us that there is only one way in which we can come out victorious and have a sense of accomplishment toward our duties without feeling worn out; and that would be in solely placing our dependency in the one true person that can help us to do it all. He asserts, "I can do all this through Him who gives me strength" (Phil. 4:13). What does this actually mean? To better understand what he is saying; let us go to the Greek Lexicon. The Greek word for *I can do* is *ischuō*, which means *to be able to do something, to have the power*[30] Our human strength can only go so far. It is God who enables us and gives us the power to endure and accomplish all that he sets us to do.

We will continue analyzing the rest of this verse. The Greek word for *through* is ἐν *(en)* which indicates the following words: in, inside, within, and in union with.[31] Doing everything in our own strength can often leave us feeling overwhelmed, unaccomplished, frustrated, disappointed and wearied; yet, when working in union with Jesus Christ, as a result we will be able to harvest inner peace, fulfillment, satisfaction, and a sense of accomplishment. When we become dependent on Christ for strength, we can achieve all that He has called us to do.

Defining your All

The question you must ask is, "What is the *all* that God has called me to achieve?" Most of us take up more than our share of loads, especially women in ministry, career women, and stay at home moms. When we do not define the *all* that God has called us to do, then we run the risk of being affected by the Do it All syndrome, such as in the cases of the following women:

Candace, a mother of two children, was an active pastor's wife who had a lot of passion in serving the Lord at her local church. She was very gifted and had many talents. She served as a worship leader, worked with women's ministry, was involved in many of the church functions, did home visitations, and also worked fulltime at the church's office. She wore many hats and could multitask, but having been able to perform so many duties and tasks all at once began to overwhelm her. She couldn't find the heart to delegate and let go of some of her tasks. Therefore, at one point, she felt burned out and her health began to deteriorate.

Maylin was a career woman who worked at a prominent business company. She was an excellent worker with a kind heart and everyone knew it. People from other departments would often ask her if she could help out in completing their tasks. This woman also did not have the heart to say no and it became a norm to for her to complete other people's jobs in addition to doing her own. After juggling so many tasks and working very long hours; she collapsed emotionally and physically. Why were these women affected by the Do it All syndrome? I believe that they spread themselves too thin and did not know how to say no. Guilt will always try to get in our way and will not allow us to say no when we know that we've reached our limits. Also, these women were so involved in multitasking that they were not able to define their God-given task or particular assignment.

Everyone has a calling in life to do a specific duty. The Lord expects us, as his children, to concentrate *only* in working toward that specific God-given task. If you do not know what it is, then it is imperative that you search it out in prayer. Usually your God-given task is connected with what drives you or what you are passionate about. If you allow Him, then He will guide you to find your special calling. He never said that it would be easy, but through His power and strength you and I can accomplish that precise *all* that has been assigned for us to do. The apostle Paul had a definite calling. He was called to preach the gospel of Jesus Christ and he knew it wasn't going to be an easy job. As he traveled he had to endure many hardships such as being thrown into prison and receiving severe beatings for the sake of fulfilling that mission. He also knew that he was not going to be able to make it by his own strength; it was only through Jesus' power that dwelled within him that enabled him to accomplish *all* that God had set forth in his life (Acts 20:23-24).

We are aware that we can multitask and that we have the capabilities of handling many functions all at once. However, allow me to say that it is not God's desire to see us overworked and overburdened. His Word tells us that He will not give us more than we can handle (1 Cor. 10:13). The Lord wants us to define our specific *all* (tasks) in order that we may not be affected by the Do it All syndrome and that we may be effective in the particular ministry or work force that He has placed us in. As His true wonder women, with His grace, wisdom and power, we will be able to conquer the world, one family at a time, one community at a time, and one task at a time.

The Effects of the Do it All Syndrome

The effects of the Do it All syndrome can cause devastating harm to our physical, emotional and spiritual being. There may be various effects; however, I have chosen to concentrate on the following two: excessive stress (and how it affects our physical and emotional health), and spiritual burnout (and how it distresses our spiritual well-being). If you are a person that is suffering from the Do it All syndrome, you are probably experiencing a deeper level of stress that can be overstretched.

Excessive Stress

The Merriam-Webster dictionary defines stress as "a state of mental tension and worry caused by problems in life, work, etc., something that causes strong feelings of worry or anxiety, physical force or pressure." How can we get rid of stress? Unfortunately, stress is inevitable. We cannot avoid it. In life we will encounter all kinds of pressures that will cause us to stress out. Some people can work great under pressure but there are others that cannot. When we do not make an effort to bring down our stress level, we may reach a point where our nervous system and physical bodies may collapse, causing damage to our health.

Doctors assert that excessive stress can produce physical and emotional effects such as high blood pressure, diabetes, depression, anxiety, bodily aches, pains, and much more. In order to avoid this kind of harmful stress, it is imperative to make some changes in our lives. When we begin to get sick because of excessive stress, we ought to consider prioritizing our obligations and duties with work, career, ministry and so forth. It is vital that we take time to care for ourselves and reduce the amount of stress that can harm our whole well-being.

Spiritual Burnout

Another effect of the Do it All syndrome can be spiritual burnout. Malcom Smith, in his book, *"Spiritual Burnout -When Doing All You Can Isn't Enough,"* defines spiritual burnout as follows: "…someone in a state of fatigue or frustration brought about by devotion to a cause, a way of life, or relationship, that failed to produce the expected reward. The man or woman who does not reach for the top will never suffer from burnout; it is a condition found only among those who want the best!"[32] Spiritual burnout can affect those who are over-achievers concerning their careers and ministries.

Serving the Lord and fulfilling His calling is a privilege and a blessing; however, at times the burden of serving can be challenging for a minister, pastor, pastor's wife, church leader or laity who is involved in church ministry. Many have felt burnout due to overloaded work duties or feel that the trials they face are too great. During these times, strength and a renewal in the spirit are much needed. Such was the case of a certain biblical superhero called Elijah; he was a man of tremendous faith and a prophet among the people of Israel. The book of 1 Kings narrates the marvelous events that took place and documents all of the long and arduous work relating to his ministry.

Let's do a quick overview of this story from chapter eighteen. Because the people of Israel turned to other gods, Elijah decided to host a large scale challenge on Mount Carmel to see whose god was real. King Ahab and all of his false prophets tried to put up a show proving that their god, Baal, was the real deal. They failed. God's fire came down from Heaven and burned down the sacrifice at the altar, proving to them that He alone was the one true God; all four hundred fifty false prophets were annihilated by order of Elijah. Afterwards, through the power of the Lord, Elijah outran, on foot, King Ahab's chariot to the city of Jezreel, which was a distance of fourteen miles, and still had to withstand the threats of the king's evil wife Jezebel, and so he fled for his life. Talk about a serious spiritual burnout. All of these incidents took a toll on him physically, mentally, and spiritually. It caused Elijah to be in a state of exhaustion and depression.

The Bible describes his overwhelming feelings of despair. It reads, "Elijah was afraid and ran for his life. When he came to Beersheba in Judah, he left his servant there, while he himself went a day's journey into the desert. He came to a broom tree, sat down under it and prayed that he might die. "I have had enough, Lord," he said. "Take my life; I am no better than my ancestors" (1 Kings 19:3-4). God then sent an angel to minister to him; he needed rest for his troubled soul and food to nourish his weary body. Elijah had run out of gas physically, emotionally and spiritually. Many of us are running like Elijah with spiritual empty tanks, worn-out and drained due to spiritual burnout. If you are experiencing any of this, our Lord is ready to send an angel to your rescue. You do not have to die in your desert. He has a plan for your life and He understands that as humans, we go through times of spiritual burnout, due to our super busy lives and laden work. Today, Jesus is inviting you to abandon a lifestyle that embraces a Do it All Syndrome and to rest in His wonderful hands.

How Can We Beat the Do it All Syndrome?

My father has a saying that is quite true. He says, "Everything in this life has a remedy, except death." Hectic schedules can be changed, trials and crisis are temporary, and there is nothing impossible for God to do. Are there any mountains that are too impossible to climb? How can we beat and overcome the Do it All Syndrome that is affecting our health and well-being? The Lord always has a solution for all our problems. Back in my university days, I learned a valuable lesson from Dr. Roger Heuser who was one of my professors. He taught us that whenever life, work, ministry, careers and trials overwhelm us, we must practice the concept of the three *R's,* which are to *Retreat, Renew* and *Return.*[33] In doing so, we can obtain rest and relief for our weary minds, souls, and bodies. Let us review this concept.

Retreat

When Elijah was told that Jezebel, his rival, was out to kill him, he ran into the desert, afraid for his life (1 Kings 19:3). There are times when our peace of mind and our spiritual, mental, and physical health are threatened by the enemy of our souls, and by the harsh things we deal with in our everyday lives. Some of these trials may be a troubled marriage, disobedient children, family quarrels, insensitive bosses and peers at work, financial hardships, health and relationship issues, overloaded work schedules, and so forth. There will also be moments in our lives when overwhelming feelings may take over and we wish we could run away like Elijah did. Unfortunately, our responsibilities do not allow us to escape into an actual desert, hoping to find an oasis.

If you're having an Elijah moment, God wants to create that special haven in the middle of your busy life. You don't have to run away from it all but you can enjoy a hideaway of your own by making time in your busy schedule to retreat. A synonym for retreat is the word *withdrawal.* We can withdraw from a stressful position or those things that bring us anxiety for a short time, in order to create a retreat that will refresh our souls. Elijah retreated from a situation that caused him an extreme amount of stress. After traveling a day's journey into the desert, Elijah found himself a broom bush as a place of shelter to rest, pray and sleep (1 Kings 19:4). The Scriptures tell us that there is a time for everything (Eccles. 3:1). We can make the time to withdraw for a moment from our hectic schedules to breath, pray, meditate in His Word, sing in our showers, laugh out loud, sleep in, get extra rest, and spoil ourselves with that desert we like from time to time, and enjoy all of His blessings. Retreats are meant to reinvigorate us and renew our strength and focus. I recommend that you go on a getaway. If you do not have the financial means to go on a luxurious vacation, you can always appoint a place at home and create your own peaceful environment where you can find rest for your body, mind and soul. Your retreat can be your bedroom, your soak tub, or even your favorite coffee shop. The point is that you find a place where you can make it your own special retreat.

Renew

When we are tired we can lose our focus and concentration. Our minds and bodies can become sluggish and even our moods and spirits are affected. Exhaustion got a hold of Elijah but the Lord sustained him. He was able to be renewed physically and spiritually by resting, sleeping and eating (1 Kings 19:5-8). If we want to be effective in our God-given tasks and be able to care for others, we must first take time to nourish ourselves by resting and getting enough sleep, and also eating nutritious foods in order that our bodies can be renewed. Our souls and body can also be renewed when doing the following: Praying, Forgiving, Freeing your Mind, take some leisure time and rest.

A: *Praying*

Jesus set the ultimate example on how to obtain spiritual renewal. He spent three long, busy years traveling from city to city, preaching, teaching, healing the sick, ministering to the poor, and setting people free from demonic possession. In spite of his busy schedule, he often retreated to *pray*. The sixth chapter of the book of Mark recounts how He fed over five thousand people, but that after ministering to them, He went away to pray (Mrk. 6:30-46). I can imagine that the human side of Jesus must have felt some exhaustion from a day's work in ministry, but he often made it a priority to make time to be with the Father. He knew that in order for him to gain divine strength and power, he had to spent time alone with Him.

Every superhero acquires his or her strong suit from someone or something superior. As God's true wonder women, our source of celestial forte comes only from the Lord. When we seek the Lord in prayer and follow His Word, His Holy Spirit strengthens our minds, hearts and spirits. Not only can we be renewed spiritually through prayer, but our souls can receive deliverance from unforgiveness.

B. *Forgiving*

We can also be renewed in our inner being when we surrender our hurts to Christ and empty our hearts from the toxic waste of bitterness and lack of forgiveness. As long as we live on this planet we will receive offenses, some intentional and others unintentional. I have served in ministry for thirty years now and have obtained my share of offenses. One thing I have learned whenever I have been offended by someone is to make time to cry it all out to God and forgive my offender as soon as possible, so that my heart can stay clean from the bacteria of resentment.

Jesus admonishes us to forgive if we want to be forgiven (Matt. 6:14). He does not ask us to forgive only when we feel like it: on the contrary, He commands us to do so at every offense. When my heart is hurting by an offense, I immediately check my busy calendar and make an appointment with God and with myself. It sounds funny, but it works for me. I say to myself, "Evie, in this particular week, you have a couple of days to cry it all out to Him, forgive, surrender, and get it out of your system. So shake it off baby and move forward!" Now, if the offense is super big, I give myself an additional time to cry some more. They say that crying flushes out the heart.

Because we are sensitive and emotional souls, sometimes it can take us longer to forgive and forget. This can produce lasting negative feelings within, such as resentment, bitterness, and lack of forgiveness; as a result, it can keep our hearts in a rut. I believe that the longer we allow ourselves to be contaminated by such emotions, the harder it will be to move forward in our Christian walk. It is the enemy's goal to keep our hearts stagnant and polluted by resentment and anger. The Lord wishes to pour Himself and His blessings into our inner being; however, He cannot fill us with his Spirit, if our hearts are full with all these poisonous feelings. We must then, surrender our brokenness, our hurts, bitterness and disappointments to Him. In return, He will generously pour out His joy, a fresh anointing, and a sense of newness in our soul; in order that we may go on experiencing His true joy and freedom in our spirit.

C. Free your mind

While retreating, likewise, it is possible that our minds can be renewed and refreshed. We can be successful in overcoming the negative thoughts that overwhelm us. How do we do this? His Word instructs us not to be anxious for anything; but rather to place our cares and petitions into God's hands. In doing so, He will give us complete renewal and peace of mind (Phil. 4:6-7). So whenever your mind is being bombarded by thoughts that will keep you in a state of worry, turn them over to Him and think only of the positive experiences that cause your heart and mind to rejoice.

D. Take Some Leisure Time and Rest

Our physical bodies can be revitalized by making time for leisure. If God rested on the seventh day after creating the world (not that He needed to), we too are expected to take a time to rest. The Lord instructed the Israelites to keep the Sabbath day; this day was meant to be God's holy day and also was designated so that His people can rest from the cares of the day (Exod. 20:8-11). We can enjoy a day of rest and leisure by doing some of the following recommendations that can produce relaxation: Take a bubble bath, a power nap, read your favorite book, go shopping, take a short vacation, or go for a coffee break with a friend. There are many other creative ways that can lead you to a leisure time; but most of all, *enjoy the things and the moments that bring you joy and peace of mind.*

Whether you're a single woman with a busy career, a student, a busy mom, or are working in ministry, it is important to make time for you. Resting will help your body to recuperate from emotional, spiritual, and physical exhaustion. As busy moms, we are always giving of ourselves to others and especially to our children; therefore, it is recommended for moms to often create a moment for leisure and rest. It can be difficult when you are raising small children, but it is not impossible. You can ask your husband, a family member, and those you trust to watch your kids for an hour or so, in order to do something special for yourself. If your toddler is napping, take advantage of this and take a small nap yourself. There are ways that make it possible for a little "Me time." It is in those little moments alone that we can hear the voice of God speak to our hearts and we are strengthened emotionally, spiritually and physically. After being renewed, we are able to return to the duties that He has called us to perform. Below, we will learn that after Elijah recuperated from his exhaustion, he returned to his post with a new anointing and fierce attitude.

Return

As Elijah was in his little hiatus inside a cave, the Lord said to him, "What are you doing here Elijah?" (1 Kings 19:9). The Lord was trying to say to him that his vacation time was over. He tells Elijah to get moving and get back to work. This superhero's assignment was not yet done. God had more amazing things to do through his life. He then was called to return to ministry. The Bible recounts that God told him to go back the same way he came into the desert, in order to complete a new mission (1 Kings 19:15-16). Our heavenly Father has a funny way of dealing with us. You would think that He would send Elijah to a better place, but no. Instead, He sends him back to the desert, which represents hardship. Elijah returned to the desert and the work field revitalized, renewed, and with a fresh new anointing. He was now able to finish his God-given task before ascending to heaven. He was sent to anoint the future kings of Syria and Israel, and also to anoint Elisha to take his place as the next prophet. Elijah also had a new boldness to confront and defeat his enemies.

The Bible tells us that his enemies tried to get him twice, but that he confronted them with a fearless faith (2 Kings 1:10-12). He experienced God's fire come down from heaven, which devoured them right in front of his eyes. "Elijah answered the captain. 'If I am a man of God, may fire come down from heaven and consume you and your fifty men!' Then fire fell from heaven and consumed the captain and his men" (v. 10). As the prophet Elijah was called to return to work, he was empowered to encounter his enemies with a superior godly confidence and courage.

It feels so good to enjoy sabbatical moments, but we can't stay hiding in our own little caves forever. If we do, we will miss out on what God has in store for us. As we retreat and renew ourselves in the Lord, just like Elijah, we too can be empowered by His Spirit to return to our duties with a new strength and a greater anointing, in order that we may victoriously overcome our trials and adversities, and succeed in our God-given tasks.

Conclusion

As women, we were made in a remarkable way. We wear a lot of hats. We are multitaskers and can perform many functions all at once. We love to give our all and beyond to our families, children, careers, ministries, friends, and communities, but there are times that we can become affected by the Do it All syndrome. Its effects can hurt our minds, bodies and spirits, causing excessive stress and a spiritual burnout. I would like to conclude this chapter by encouraging you to love yourself a little more by making some time in your busy schedule for you. Our Heavenly Father will not mind it. In fact, He encourages us to take time to rest (Mrk. 2:27). Never forget that the Lord created sabbatical moments for everyone—even for a true wonder woman such as you.

I reiterate that whenever you get caught up by the Do it All syndrome, in the middle of your busyness, you can beat it by following this formula: *retreat* in your special getaway, *renew* yourself through His Spirit in prayer and take time for leisure (it will allow you to refresh and recuperate), and then you can *return* with confidence and with a greater strength to continue on blessing others with a stronger you. Also, you will be able to keep going on fulfilling your God-given purpose and task in your journey. I invite you to join me in this prayer to receive God's special rest for your mind, body and soul.

Prayer for God's Rest

Dear Heavenly Father, I come to You exhausted from the pains and labors of this ongoing evolving world. I surrender my weariness and hurtful heart. Please restore it with Your kindness and gentle love. I throw myself in Your loving arms and in this secluded space where You and I stand alone, I receive Your special touch and rest that will produce in me inner and outer healing. In Your presence I am fully restored. Thank You for your amazing love and understanding. I realize that through You, I can accomplish all that You have called me to do with joy and peace of mind. In Jesus name I pray. Amen.

Chapter Five

"And the God of all grace, who called you to his eternal glory in Christ, after you have suffered a little while, will himself restore you and make you strong, firm and steadfast."(1Peter 5:10)

Conquering the Traumas of Sexual Abuse

Linny was a bright, talented, and cheerful child. When she was five years old, she discovered a passion for singing. She loved to sing Christian classic songs on Sunday night services, which were taught to her by her mother. Whenever she practiced her songs, she would grab a hairbrush pretending it was a microphone and imagined herself singing in a platform in front of a big audience. At the tender age of eight, she gave her heart to the Lord and received the baptism of the Holy Spirit. Linny was on fire for God. She would preach to the kids in her third grade classroom and did not care if they teased her. She attended all the prayer services and vigils, and sought the Lord with all her heart. As a child, she had many aspirations and dreams. One of her dreams was to someday become a missionary and preach the gospel of Jesus Christ.

Linny was a happy child and always had a cheerful smile on her face, but one dreadful day, an unexpected and diabolical event happened. It wiped the smile off of her heart for many years, leaving her with an emotional and spiritual wound that shattered her dreams. Linny was molested and sexually assaulted in an empty school hallway. The enemy had stricken her like a tornado does when it passes by a city; it destroys everything in its path. Consequently, this attack ripped the joy out of this young child's soul and broke her spirit. I know Linny very well and can identify myself with her pain, because the truth is that I am Linny. I was that child who was sexually violated and attacked. This is my story. Permit me to tell you a little bit more in depth about how it all happened, and how in the midst of this journey, Christ came to me and set me free from the roots of bitterness.

It was a rainy afternoon and all the children, along with their teachers, were asked to go to the school's auditorium for a school meeting with the principal. As I sat in my chair, I remember having an urge to go to the restroom. I asked for permission and the teacher gave me the OK to go by myself. I had to cross a long hallway in order to reach the girls' bathroom. I managed to get there without a care but as I was exiting the girl's room, I noticed that the hallway was empty. There were no adults around. I remember sensing an eerie feeling inside me but could not understand why. All of a sudden, two bigger boys appeared and looked at me with lust in their eyes. I heard one of them tell the other, "let's get her," and so, I ran as quickly as possible but they were much faster and stronger. They took a hold of me and sexually assaulted me in that empty school hallway.

After the attack, I ran back to my chair and was in a complete state of shock. My heart was beating very fast and feelings of fear, shame, dirt and guilt covered my mind and tiny heart. As an eight year old little girl, I was naïve, afraid and defenseless. I never told anyone what had happened to me. As a result of the incident, I suffered many nightmares during the night. I would dream that the enemy would speak to me, telling me, "It was your fault that this happened to you. You are a dirty little girl and nothing will ever be the same between you and God. You are no longer, holy in His eyes. In fact, He does not love you because He left you alone." The enemy was putting all those negative thoughts in my head and I believed him. At that time, I felt very angry with God. I told the Lord the following words, "God, where were you when this happened to me? Why didn't you protect me? Listen Lord, I promise to serve you because that's all I know how to do, and I do not wish to do anything else. However, I will never forgive you for abandoning me. Why did you let this happen to me, when I had given you my life?" In my anger and despair, I did not allow God to answer me. I then chose to forget the incident and never talked about it with Him or anyone else. Next, I buried it into a spiritual dungeon inside my inner being.

They say that time heals old wounds, but that was not necessarily true for me. I now realize that spiritual wounds do not heal over time. They need to be treated and can only be cured by the healing touch of the Master. His Word tells us that He is the healer of all those who have wounded hearts: "He heals the brokenhearted and binds up their wounds" (Ps.147:3). Among other kinds of abuses that I have faced in my life, I was a victim of sexual abuse, and because of it I lost my identity. My true self was wrapped in feelings of guilt, shame, and bitterness for a very long time. In my teenage years, I went through a very hard phase of spiritual drought. I continued to regularly attend church with my folks and tried to seek God by praying and going to all the youth functions. I was accustomed to going to church and felt that I loved the Lord, but the reality was that the spiritual part of my heart was infected and unhealthy. I knew that God was a healer, but I had not completely surrendered that internal pain that kept me in spiritual bondage. Depression would often get a hold of me, obscuring my joy and inner strength, and crushing my self-esteem. Many times, in my despair, I was oppressed by the enemy with suicidal thoughts.

A spirit of suicide and death began to attack my mind and got a hold of me. Three times, I tried to commit suicide, and in my last attempt, I had an out of body experience. I was sixteen years old at that time and I remember being alone in my room, when the enemy began to harass me, telling me that if I took my own life, the pain I felt inside would go away. At that moment, I allowed the enemy to blind my faith in God and made me think that maybe the Lord did not love me anymore because I was not worthy enough to be loved. I then made the choice to listen to the enemy's voice and took hold of a bottle of pain medication, and overdosed on them. Minutes later, I saw the spirit of death coming for me. I felt extremely weak and a coldness that covered my body. I collapsed and fell to the ground, and completely stopped breathing. I felt as if I died that day. I recollect that my spirit came out of my body and I saw myself laying cold stiff on the floor. My spirit stepped out of my room and went to the living room where my family was sitting watching TV. At that instant, they had no knowledge of what had happened to me. They thought that I was in my room studying. I tried to call them, but they could not hear or see me. I then went back to my room and as I was standing next to my body, I saw the floor open up and my soul began to descend into a dark tunnel. I knew there and then, that I was going straight to hell because as I was getting closer to the bottom of that deep and dark tunnel, I heard horrific loud voices of desperate people screaming, "Help, someone get us out of here!"

As my soul was descending, it got hotter and hotter. I began to call upon the Lord to have mercy on me and to save my life. I cried to Him and said, "Lord, please forgive me and don't let me go to hell. Please give me another chance and I promise you that I will serve you wholeheartedly!" Just before my feet touched the burning flames of hell, in the midst of my desperate cries, I saw God's hand reach out and pulled me out of that black tunnel, taking me back to my room. I stood standing in front of my body that was laying on the floor and a heavenly angel appeared and said to me, "You must go back, you've been spared and given a second chance. If you try to take your life again, you will not be given another opportunity. However, God has a divine plan for you on earth. Go forth on His path and do not deviate from it." After my soul went back into my body, I woke up feeling very weak. Soon after, my brother walked in my room and found me there lying on the floor. Right away, my parents took me to the hospital and the doctors treated me. The doctor told me that it was a miracle that I was still alive.

After that experience, I promised the Lord that I would never try to take my own life away, yet as a teen, I still hadn't completely surrendered the pain of my past. Time passed by and I grew up. I got married, entered into ministry, traveled the world, had kids, went to Bible school and theological seminary, and was very busy serving in a pastoral ministry. However, there was something holding me back from being and feeling totally free in my spirit. I needed an internal healing in my soul. The sexual abuse that I had suffered as a child produced a deep wound in my heart and I never cared to treat it. I had been carrying a sad little girl with an emotional injury inside the deepest part of my soul for many years. As a result of holding on to that hurt for such a long time, the emotional wound became filled with the spiritual pus of resentment and unforgiveness; it created in me roots of bitterness. I was not aware that these roots of bitterness had entangled my womb and preventing me from truly enjoying Christ's freedom in the spirit, and from growing spiritually as God had intended for me. I was obstructed from fulfilling my true potential.

A deep sense of insecurity, shame, and fear had always attacked my mind and self-esteem. Therefore, I felt that I was never progressing emotionally, until one Thursday night. As I was taking a shower, a spirit of fear arose, attacking my thoughts, and so I began to rebuke it. I finally realized that I needed deliverance inside of me. I recollect making a prayer to God:

Heavenly Father, I ask you to please set me free once and for all from whatever spiritual and emotional bondage I may be holding inside my soul. I do not recognize what I'm carrying within me, but I definitely know that something is wrong and that I need deliverance in my spirit. I surrender my whole being to you. Lord, can you come to me and touch my heart? I do not wish anyone to pray over me. I only want to feel your hands healing me. Please set me free, in Jesus name.

After the abuse, I became fearful and seldom allowed people to lay hands on me. I did not like anyone touching me. Due to the fact that I had buried that horrible incident inside my subconscious, I could not remember all the details and the things I said to God during the time of my assault; furthermore, I could not recollect my feelings of anger and unforgiveness toward my assaulters. To my understanding, I was done with that issue and felt that since many years had gone by, there was no benefit in remembering the past. I asked the Lord to set me free on a Thursday night. Two days passed by, and I had not received an answer. At first, I thought that He had not heard my prayers, but I kept waiting on Him. Scripture tells us that God hears the prayers of his people and is always willing to deliver us: "When the righteous cry for help, the Lord hears and delivers them out of all their troubles. The Lord is near to the brokenhearted and saves the crushed in spirit" (Ps. 34:17-18, ESV).

My deliverance came on the following Sunday night at a prayer service. I clearly recall that the power of God was moving in a mighty way. My husband was playing the keyboard and had made an altar call. As the people began to pray wholeheartedly, an outpouring of the Holy Spirit began to descend upon us. Many fell to the ground without anyone touching them. They were receiving deliverance and healing. I was standing at the right hand side of the altar alongside with the worship team. As I saw people receive blessings, I asked God, "Lord, what about me?" Immediately, my husband who was playing the keyboard across the other side of the altar, looked straight into my eyes and said, "Evie, tonight God will set you free. Receive your deliverance!" It was amazing because he had no knowledge of my abuse and of my prayer to God for deliverance. I had not shared the incident with him or anyone else. As soon as he spoke those words, I felt the power of the Holy Spirit touch me and I instantly fell to the floor. No one had prayed over me. It was the Lord himself that came to visit me.

While I lay on the altar floor, my spiritual eyes were opened. I saw the hand of God that entered and reached into the deepest part of my womb and pulled out a sad little girl. To my surprise, this sad little girl was me. I saw myself as the wounded child that had suffered sexual abuse when I was eight years old. When I saw that vision of my young hurtful self, staring straight at me with a look of depression on her face, I sensed a creepy feeling in my heart. I felt as if I were in a horror movie. Instantaneously, I witness how God began to erase her image with his hand and in seconds the sad and broken little child no longer existed within me. I was relieved to see her gone and thought all was well, but the Lord was not done with me yet. There were still some more bondages inside me that needed to be cut off from their roots. After God had removed Linny, as I like to call her, He said to me,

"If you want to be set free completely, you must forgive the assaulters that attacked you that day in the school hallway."

In this vision, He then proceeded to take me back to the incident where the kids took a hold of me. It felt as if I was watching a movie of myself. As I witnessed the frightful event, it stirred up the old feelings of anger and hate I had kept toward my offenders. I never knew those boys that attacked me, but there and then, I saw their faces and decided that I was finally going to deal with the pain and hide it no more. In this vision, I looked straight in their eyes and said to them, "I forgive you wholeheartedly. I will no longer hold you captive with resentment and anger inside my heart. I release you to God."

Suddenly, I saw the hand of the Lord heal the wound that was still opened in my heart. I unconsciously lived with a bleeding heart for all those years, but now the Lord had come to heal it. Still, He was not done with me. He continued on, saying, "Do you want to be set free completely?" I replied, "Yes Lord." He said, "You must surrender all your anger and resentment that you have had against me throughout these past years. You thought that I abandoned you at the time of the attack, but the reality is different from what you remember. Let me show you what really happened. One of the boys had a pocket knife and was going to stab you but I sent an angel to protect you. As soon as they heard the footsteps of my angel passing by the hallway, they thought that someone was coming and so they got scared and ran off. I know that you think that it isn't fair that I allowed this to happen to you, but I spared you from the worst. The enemy might have caused an inflicting wound in your spirit, but his aim was to kill you. I saved you from death, and as you receive your inner healing, one day you will be able to tell women who have endured the same hurt that there is an ultimate healer that can heal the heart and restore their lives completely." With contrition, I asked God to forgive me for being angry at him and I thanked him for saving my life that day. Afterwards, I watched His hand go inside my belly one last time and pull out a humongous root stem that looked as if it was one hundred yards long.

The Lord had torn away the spiritual roots of bitterness that were entwined deep inside my womb for so long. Soon after, He generously poured a special anointing on my head that flowed throughout my whole entire being. God not only set me free from spiritual bondage and the effects of the trauma from the sexual abuse; but more so, He filled me with a fresh anointing of His Holy Spirit that changed my life completely. I am not only a survivor of sexual abuse; I am a victor through Jesus Christ and not a victim of Satan anymore. As His true wonder woman, I have discovered that through His power, I can rise above it all. If you are a victim of sexual abuse, you do not have to live in a state of shame and brokenness. God is a God of restoration. If He renewed my inner being, He can do it for you too, only if you allow Him to do so. We might not understand why these kinds of things happen, however we must remember that while we live in this world, We will not be exempt from suffering emotional and physical wounds. Christ suffered pain, sorrow, and the agony of the cross for our sins. The apostle Peter tells us not to be surprised at the fact that we too have to endure hurts and pain, but rather, we must rejoice in partaking in Christ's sufferings (1 Pet. 4:12-13).

There are emotional, psychological and most of all spiritual ramifications from sexual abuse. When it comes to the spiritual part, there are many people out there and even Christians that are skeptical in believing that Satan can put these victims in a spiritual bondage and oppress them. After experiencing deliverance over the traumas of sexual abuse, I can truly say that when we surrender our hurts and wounds to God, he heals our brokenness, sets us free completely from all the spiritual chains, and empowers us to live victoriously.

I have served in ministry for over thirty years in different areas, including pastoral ministry, and the Lord has allowed me to minister to women who have suffered sexual abuse. As a result, I have witnessed how they too have been set free from their traumas and even from demonic oppression. After learning the staggering numbers of statistics of rape victims worldwide and in our own nation, the Lord put it in my heart to include this chapter with the purpose of not only sharing my own personal experience of how God set me free, but also give victims of sexual abuse both hope and guidance on how to receive deliverance for their spirit. I would like to thank my husband for encouraging me to write about this subject that is most needed. In this chapter, we will be addressing the effects and ramifications of sexual abuse, how the enemy comes to bind and oppress his victims and most importantly, how we can be set free. It is my ultimate intention to convey a positive message to women that have been sexually abused. I'd like to say that there is hope and that the healing power of Jesus Christ can bring a full restoration to a wounded soul. You can conquer the traumas of sexual abuse and discover the true wonder women in you with the help of the Holy Spirit.

What is Sexual Assault?

To be sexually assaulted indicates that someone has forced them self upon you, violating your body in a sexual manner and touching your body parts without your consent. The organization, Safe Horizon, defines sexual assault as follows: "Sexual assault is a general term that includes any forced or unwanted sexual activity, including rape, incest, sexual abuse, and molestation. Sexual assault includes any forced or unwanted touching of an intimate part of the body, such as breast, buttock, or genitals."[34] Sexual abuse, or any kind of abuse, is not to be tolerated or excused. In continuation, we will observe how this type of crime was also committed in the Bible times.

Rape & Incest in the Bible Times

Sexual abuse is caused by evil people who are used by Satan to commit acts of wickedness and violence against others. It is not a crime caused by God and we are not to blame Him. Acts such as these have roots since the beginning of time. In the Old Testament, we find a compelling tale of a beautiful princess named Tamar, daughter of King David, who was a victim of sexual abuse and incest. She was raped by her step brother. Her story is told in (2 Sam. 13:1-22).

Tamar's brother, Amnon, was in love with his sister but it was not a pure, brotherly love. He was lusting over her to the point that his sexual depravity was tormenting him. Amnon pretended to be ill and asked his father, King David, if his sister Tamar could come over to his house and make him some bread. Unaware of his son's intentions, King David granted his wish and sent his daughter over to her brother's home. When she got there, she baked him the bread and gave it to him, but he wasn't interested. He requested that his servants and all those around leave them alone and asked Tamar to bring the bread to his bedroom. Tamar was also unaware of her brother's intentions. When she took the bread to him, the Bible says that he took advantage of her and grabbed her (v. 11). She begged him not to rape her, but his lust and wickedness was greater than his love for her.

Tamar was not only violated but was put in a state of shame and isolation. If a woman lost her virginity before marriage, according to the laws of Israel back in those days, she was considered to be disgraced and isolated from society for life with no chances of getting a suitor for marriage. Sexual abuse is a crime that is committed by perverted people. Many women of the past have suffered because of it, and it still happens today to countless women. The statistics below confirm the widespread occurrence of such horrendous acts toward women and children.

Statistics

Unfortunately, many sexually abused victims find it hard to express their trauma due to shame and emotional distress. Because of this factor, it is impossible to accurately obtain a true percentage of victims; however, there are organizations nationwide and also worldwide that are dedicated to reaching out and helping women and children who have encountered this kind of violence. These organizations can provide us with some statistics concerning this matter.

Worldwide

Like me, there are many women worldwide that have suffered this kind of abuse, whether by a stranger, boyfriend, relative, or friend. According to the World Health Organization, there are a great percentage of women who have encountered sexual abuse. The following are some of their statistics:

"Between 15% of women in Japan and 71% of women in Ethiopia reported physical and/or sexual violence by an intimate partner in their lifetime; Between 0.3–11.5% of women reported experiencing sexual violence by someone other than a partner since the age of 15 years; The first sexual experience for many women was reported as forced – 17% of women in rural Tanzania, 24% in rural Peru, and 30% in rural Bangladesh reported that their first sexual experience was forced. A more recent analysis of WHO with the London School of Hygiene and Tropical Medicine and the Medical Research Council, based on existing data from over 80 countries, found that globally 35% of women have experienced either physical and/or sexual intimate partner violence or non-partner sexual violence. Most of this violence is intimate partner violence. Worldwide, almost one third (30%) of all women who have been in a relationship have experienced physical and/or sexual violence by their intimate partner, in some regions this is much higher."[35]

The statistics show that there are many women around the world that have suffered from sexual abuse. More than ever, we must pray for the victims, that the Lord may bring healing and restoration to their lives and we must also pray that the Lord will convict all perpetrators and bring them to repentance. Our world needs healing and salvation. We must pray for Christ's light to shine in this world of darkness.

Nationwide

It is sad to say that here in our own home land, the United States; women are being victimized by the same violence. The National Center for Injury Prevention and Control has provided a survey with an alarming number of statistics of American women and children who have suffered sexual abuse within the United State:

"In a nationally representative survey of adults:1 Nearly 1 in 5 (18.3%) women and 1 in 71 men (1.4%) reported experiencing rape at some time in their lives. (College Age) 37.4% of female rape victims were first raped between ages 18-24.1 (Children and Youth) 42.2% of female rape victims were first raped before age 18. 29.9% of female rape victims were first raped between the ages of 11-17. 12.3% female rape victims and 27.8% of male rape victims were first raped when they were age 10 or younger"[36]

The statistics are disturbing and also helps us to be aware of what's happening here in our own nation. Violence and sexual assault toward women and children have increased. This news puts us in high alert that now more than ever; we ought to cover our children, sisters, relatives and friends in prayer for protection and for healing for those who have suffered such abuse. We will now look further at some of the effects of sexual abuse.

Effects

The effects from sexual abuse can be overwhelming and traumatizing emotionally, psychologically, spiritually, and physically. It is imperative that we acknowledge the aftermath of sexual abuse in order to learn how to deal with the outcomes, and how to seek the appropriate help. Let us take a look at the multiple negative effects of sexual abuse.

Physical Effects

Victims of sexual abuse can suffer physical effects, such as being exposed to STD. Dr. Traci C. Johnson defines STD and gives some recommendations on how to treat it:

"Sexually transmitted diseases, commonly called STDs, are diseases that are spread by having sex with someone who has an STD. You can get a sexually transmitted disease from sexual activity that involves the mouth, anus, vagina, or penis. STDs are serious illnesses that require treatment. Some STDs, like HIV, cannot be cured and are deadly. By learning more, you can find out ways to protect yourself from the following STDs. Genital herpes, Human papilloma virus/Genital warts, Hepatitis B, Chlamydia, Syphilis, Gonorrhea ("Clap"). Many STDs are treated with antibiotics. If you are given an antibiotic to treat an

STD, it's important that you take all of the drug, even if the symptoms go away. Also, never take someone else's medicine to treat your illness. By doing so, you may make it more difficult to diagnose and treat the infection.[37]"

Other effects of sexual abuse can be physical pains and injuries in the body or genitals. Victims can also suffer from an unwanted pregnancy. If you have suffered a rape, I strongly recommend that you go to your local clinic and get examined by a doctor right away and seek treatment.

Emotional and Psychological Effects

Countless victims feel a great amount of guilt, shame, fear, insecurity, anxiety, or depression, or experience difficulty in having intimacy with their spouse, or suffer from other effects. They may find it difficult to trust people and can often become extremely overprotective with their own children. They may also fear to be alone or in crowds, thinking that they will be attacked again. In some cases, there are women who contemplate committing suicide. Their sense of value and sense of worth is diminished, and they also experience self-condemnation. The emotional and psychological effects can be so powerful, that there are women that manifest their fear, guilt, and shame by developing unhealthy habits.

Some will find comfort in food, smoking, drugs, or illicit sex; develop eating disorders and many other addictions in order to hide their pain. Those who turn to food, as a result, put on weight. Such was the case of Valerie, a woman I met in a health class back in college. I had taken that class in order to learn more about nutrition and how to eat better. The dietician asked the class the following: "What is your motivation to learn more about eating healthier?" Valerie replied, "I was raped last year. Due to the violation, I suppressed my hurtful emotions and use food as a crutch. I am now fifty pounds overweight and at first I felt secure, thinking that no one will rape me anymore because I am fat and unattractive; however, the excess weight is affecting my health and I know that I need to lose it." Thankfully, this woman sought the right help and she was on her way to a total recovery from the emotional effects of sexual abuse. By the end of the semester, she had lost most of the weight.

Dealing with the psychological and spiritual ramifications from a sexual trauma is vital for a complete inner healing. We can learn to cope, deal and overcome the emotional scars of sexual abuse. However, if we do not also acknowledge its spiritual outcomes, we will not receive a true recovery.

How am I affected spiritually?

Because of the shame produced by sexual abuse, many women hide their hurt and prefer to keep it as a deep secret. When we do not deal with the issue, seek counseling, surrender the pain to God, and forgive the assaulter, we open our hearts to anger, resentment, and roots of bitterness develop within our spirits, producing a spiritual bondage. The spiritual outcome of rape and sexual assault can be manifested in different ways. Some women experience an extreme amount of fear, guilt, and self-condemnation. Others develop an appetite for lust or illicit sex, and may become promiscuous. That is why it is important for the victim of sexual abuse to not only receive emotional and psychological help, but also to seek spiritual intervention.

Transferable Spirits

Could it be possible that evil spirits be transferred through intercourse? Many of us know that sexually transmitted diseases or viruses can be transmitted through sexual contact. In the same manner, spirits can also be transferrable through sexual intercourse. The Bible tells us that when we unite ourselves sexually with a prostitute or worldly person, through sexual intercourse, we become one body and one flesh (1 Cor. 6:15-16). There have been cases where women who have been raped have been affected by the assailant's spirit.

Analia had come to me for prayer for deliverance. She was raped by a family member. The man that raped her had a spirit of lust. This young woman confessed that after being raped, she developed a craving for sex and became addicted to it; as a result she started sleeping around with many different men. If for some reason, you are facing lustful cravings or addictions that were not there before, due to a rape by a depraved man, there is hope. God is a God of love and loves us no matter what life has thrown our way. His love for us does not change.

We are assured in the book of Romans that no "…distress, tribulation, persecution, famine, nakedness, danger or sword can separate us from the love of Christ." (Rom. 8:35). He died for our sins, so that we could live freely from it. We do not have to live entrapped by our sinful cravings and allow them to dictate our walk. It is God's desire to heal our inner wounds and set us free from any sinful bondage that will lead us to live a destructive life. If you have been a victim of sexual abuse, it is imperative that you seek counseling, prayer and a comprehensive spiritual deliverance. In doing so, this will aid and guide you to receive a total liberation in your spirit, mind, and soul from the psychological, emotional, and spiritual outcomes of sexual abuse.

How to Receive Restoration

The Lord is in the business of restoring the brokenhearted and creating newness in the lives of his people. He hurts when we hurt, and as the God of joy he longs to see us smile and rejoice wholeheartedly again. In the book of Jeramiah, the Lord tells His people who were once outcasts and in bondage from the Babylonians that He would restore them completely. Our Heavenly Father also wants to restore our hearts, minds, and souls entirely (Jer. 30:17). So let us take a hold of His promises for healing and restoration. How can we receive complete restoration? Let's examine the process.

Recognize, Confess, & Seek Help

The first step one must take in order to obtain a complete restoration from the effects of sexual abuse is to recognize that there is an internal problem. Because of shame, I have seen many women fear to talk about their past because it hurts and they are in a state of denial. While they are suffering from the emotional and spiritual effects of sexual abuse, they come for prayer and counseling only to ease their pain. However, some do not receive complete inner healing because they do not admit that they truly have a problem that must be dealt with. The beginning of healing starts with a confession. The Bible says: "Therefore confess your sins to each other and pray for each other so that you may be healed" (Jm. 5:16).

A person who has suffered rape or sexual assault has been violated and a sin has been committed toward that person. If we keep that offense a secret in our hearts without coming forward with our pain, then we remain trapped in our deepest hurts and we will not receive complete inner healing. It is important for us to seek professional and spiritual counseling if we've been abused. I encourage you to not be afraid to open up your heart to someone you trust and feel confident enough to share your hurt with. It can be a doctor, a counselor, your pastor, pastor's wife, or a spiritual leader that can guide you through the healing process.

Seek God

Many of us look to different forms of relief to ease our internal pain. Victims of sexual abuse often turn to all kinds of addictions and obsessions such as food, illicit sex, work and other strange devices. As a victim myself, I have realized that nothing can take the place of God to relieve inner pain. Jesus understands us. He understands our pain and he sympathizes with our hurts. He himself suffered a great amount of emotional and physical pain while he was here on earth. The prophet Isaiah described Jesus as a "Man of sorrows and familiar with sufferings" (Isa. 53:3). Christ died with a bleeding heart for us, but he resurrected with great power as a great conqueror.

The Bible tells us that Christ conquered death. In Jesus we are more than conquerors, and through him we can experience a love that overcomes our pain, sorrow and heartaches (Rom. 6:9). In his love we can rest, assured that our grief is no match for the peace that he willingly offers when we come to him with our hurts in hand. Only Jesus can mend the brokenness caused by sexual abuse and only his love can erase its sting, but we cannot experience the fullness of his peace if we do not seek Him. Avoiding Jesus in our worst moments can only lead to more distress, and I encourage you to run to Him because He knows how you feel. Run to the one who shares in your sorrows. Seek the Lord and you will discover that your hurt of sexual abuse will soon disappear.

Choose Forgiveness over Un-forgiveness

Forgiveness is made possible through Jesus Christ who shed his blood for us at Calvary. He forgave us from all of our sins and wrongdoings, so it is important for us to learn how to forgive others, even if it hurts. You might think that forgiveness may do nothing for your offender but it does a whole lot for you and your soul. Forgiveness brings freedom to our spirits; however, un-forgiveness can cause consequences to our souls. Allow me to point out what happens to us when we choose not to forgive our trespassers. First of all, when we are not willing to forgive, we are putting ourselves in God's place. We become judges. When we choose not to forgive our offenders, we are holding their offense deep in our hearts and we begin thinking about all the horrible things we wish would happen to them and all the bad things we think that they deserve. Spiritually, we are taking God's place as a judge who deals with people and their crimes in his own time and by his own wisdom. Remember, we are not judges.

Un-forgiveness does not allow God to do his job of healing our hearts, if we spend all our time plotting revenge in our minds or creating our own versions of justice. James tells us that there is only one judge in this world and that is God. He is the only one able to correct or punish a transgressor (Jm. 4:12). We have not been given the authority to judge anyone.

Second, un-forgiveness poisons our hearts. Its effects cover our inner being with a spiritual toxic waste, such as bitterness, anger, anxiety, fear, and resentment. Scripture tells us to keep our souls clean and pure, loving our neighbor with a pure heart (1 Pet. 1:22). When we don't empty our hearts from these toxic spiritual wastes, we start to wake up with these feelings on a daily basis, and sooner or later they become a normal part of our everyday lives. God does not want us to live like this; He wants us to live with the freedom to experience joy, love, peace, and happiness. We cannot experience positive feelings if we dwell on negativity from the moment we wake up until the moment we go to sleep. Third, we withhold ourselves from receiving forgiveness when we sin against others. The Bible tells us how our Heavenly Father reacts toward our attitude concerning forgiveness for our debtors (Matt. 6:14-15). Just as He forgave our sins, He expects for us to do the same toward our transgressors. If we do not, He in return will also not forgive our sins. I know it's not easy, as a victim of sexual abuse, to forgive your offender; trust me, it took me years to forgive the boys who assaulted me. But I learned that forgiveness can set us free.

If we surrender our pain to God and allow Him to soothe our hearts with his love, He in return will give us the strength to forgive others. Fourth, un-forgiveness causes spiritual incarceration and demonic oppression. In the book of Matthew, Jesus spoke about the story of a Master who forgave his servant's debt and how his servant, after being forgiven, chose not to forgive his own servant who owed him a much lesser debt. This cruel man had no mercy and had his own servant thrown in jail (Matt. 18:21-35). When the master found out what this first servant did, he was outraged by his injustice. In verse thirty-four, we read that "the master handed him over to the jailers to be tortured." If we do not forgive, as I said before, our Lord will not forgive us; and as a result, we make the choice to live outside of His protection over our minds and hearts, and we become susceptible to the torment of evil spirits.

Un-forgiveness opens a door for the enemy to oppress us and torture us when we hold resentment in our hearts. A victim of sexual abuse never forgets what happened in the past. When we dwell on the hurtful event, emotionally, it slowly eats us alive. The devil never lets us have a moment's peace. If we start to forget, he's always there to remind us of it and of our pain; more so, to torture us with the thought of reliving the event. That is oppression. It only continues if we choose to live in un-forgiveness, but the Lord is ever so gentle with us when we are in pain and when we choose to wallow in it. He is patient with us when we find it difficult to forgive and gives us a constant reminder of His love when we feel like we won't make it. He is waiting for us to come to him with our struggles so that He may empower us to do what we never thought we could do, which is to forgive the ones who hurt us in the worst way. Let us not take un-forgiveness lightly. Remember that the consequences of un-forgiveness last a lifetime and God does not want us to spend our precious life living in anger, resentment, hurt, and in a state of demonic oppression.

Forgiveness Brings Healing and Freedom

True forgiveness of the heart will bring true freedom and inner healing. There's no room in our hearts for God's love when we chose to live in resentment. However, if we empty ourselves before Him, allowing him to pick up our broken pieces, we can experience a healing that restores our emotions and fills the core of our spirit with the peace we have been yearning for. He cares about our emotional wounds as well as our physical being. The Bible says that Jesus loved us so much that He carried our sorrows **(Isa. 53:4)**. In the book of 1 Peter, we find that He was wounded in order that we may receive healing: "...by his wounds you have been healed." (2:24).

Because Jesus experienced pain and was wounded by the world, he is the one who is qualified to heal all of our wounds; body and soul. When we decide to take the leap of forgiving our offenders, we are clearing our hearts of hate and hurt; consequently, clearing a path for God to work in us and give us the restoration we are looking for. We also are no longer holding our transgressor captive emotionally and spiritually within us. Forgiveness releases them to God, so that He can judge them according to their doings. Forgiveness is for our benefit, as the victims. The benefits of forgiveness are rewarding. It sets us free from the bondage of resentment and bitterness. It also gives us a sense of health and well-being. Our spirits feel lighter and not heavy from the yoke of un-forgiveness. We are free to love and our hearts are clear and ready to receive God's newness.

Moving Forward

Our hurtful past will never be forgotten because the incidents are recorded in our minds. Our minds are like a computer filled with data. When the information is stored in the computer, it is available. One can have access to its data at any time. Recollections of our hurtful past will resurface in our minds from time to time; it is inevitable because the enemy still wants to use our past to bring us down on a daily basis. However, the best part about using God's strength to help us forgive the ones who hurt us is the part when we finally are able to forget the pain of the traumatic event.

When we forgive our enemies with all our hearts and allow God to fill in the gaps that pain has left us with, we can remember the event but the feelings of hurt disappear! You no longer have to fight an emotional battle every time the crime of sexual assault is brought up. You are free from the feelings that were attached to the memory and you are able to move forward in peace. **This is how I am able to share my testimony without any pain: I have found the strength in Christ to forgive my trespassers, and have been able to move forward.** We must be aware that while living here on earth, we will all experience some kind of painful wilderness. The question is: Do we stay in the desert of pain or do we choose to move forward? We are encouraged by Paul not to look back, but to move forward in pursuing God's ultimate glory for us (Phil. 3:13-14).

Recently, as I was going through a transition in ministry, I was feeling a little sad and at the same time hurt by some painful experiences I had endured. I knew in my heart that I had to forgive and move on because in the end, those bad experiences were going to be something of the past. However, sometimes the unhappy memories would overwhelm my mind. One day, the Lord spoke to me and said, "You must not think of things that make you sad. Forget the past and move forward." Eventually, I was able to overcome the sad thoughts and I understood that no matter how painful some experiences are in life, there is always something that we can learn from our pain. Nevertheless, if we want to grow, we must shift our focus from our hurtful memories and concentrate on God and his plans for us.

There is a purpose for the good and bad in our lives. The good helps us to strive for greater things and the bad helps us to grow in ways we never thought we could. I once thought that nothing good would come from my experience of sexual abuse, but here I am, stronger and wiser than I've ever been before. I'm fully equipped to serve and help those who are suffering just as I have suffered, because I've been there before and I know that victory over sexual trauma is possible with the help of Jesus Christ. Let us move on to the next chapter in our lives, accepting both the good and the bad and stepping out in faith toward the greater things that God has in store for us. Our Heavenly Father would like you to understand that there are bigger stories to be written on the blank pages of your heart: larger waves to ride in the sea of life, greater miracles to experience, and countless blessings to obtain as you move forward. Keep in mind that the enemy uses the hurts of our past to hold us back from experiencing the newness that God is creating.

In the book of Isaiah the Lord told the Israelites who had to endured slavery not to dwell on their past because He was creating something new; something bigger and better for their lives. When we dwell on the painful experiences of the past, we get stuck there and ultimately miss out on witnessing what God is about to do in us and through us. Listen with your heart to what the Lord is telling you: "Forget the former things; do not dwell on the past. See, I am doing a new thing! Now it springs up; do you not perceive it?" **(Isa. 43:18-19)**. So whenever the enemy brings back the aching and sad thoughts that bring you down, reject them in Jesus' name and believe that the Lord is on the move to creating a whole new life for you filled with His bountiful blessings. I encourage you to courageously move forward toward conquering the effects of sexual abuse. This will lead you one step closer in discovering the true wonder woman in you.

Conclusion

I would like to reiterate that sexual abuse is a result of sin and God is not to be blamed for it. Statistics show that one in six women have been violated. The statistics of sexual abuse are alarming, as thousands of women and children are sexually assaulted in this country. The effects of sexual abuse can be traumatic. If you are a victim of sexual abuse, you can receive deliverance by surrendering your hurts and pains to the Lord and by forgiving your trespassers. God promises restoration for broken people. Jesus died at the cross so that we may obtain salvation for our souls and also healing for our bodies, minds, hearts and spirit.

God's renewal makes us strong in faith, hope and love. Embrace his renewal of the spirit and you will no longer walk as a victim but as a victor. In Christ you are a winner and can conquer it all. So go ahead, lift up your hands to heaven in gladness, dare to dream again, sing, and dance. There's a new day coming for you. His renewal is at your doorstep. All you have to do is open the door and let Jesus come into your heart and allow him to do the impossible in your life. He would like to give you a new song to sing. Sing a tune of victory in Jesus Christ (Ps. 30:11-12).

Prayer for Restoration

Heavenly Father, I come to You as a broken vessel in need of restoration. I also come to You with a bleeding heart and a wounded soul. Lord, you are a God that restores the broken and can make all things new. I ask that, as I surrender my heart, mind, and soul to You; You would renew my entire inner being, heal my wounds, set me free from the chains and bondage of unforgiveness and make me whole again. From the bottom of my heart, I forgive my offenders and release them to You. May Your Holy Spirit cleanse and purify me. Please set me free and fill me with Your presence. In Jesus name, I ask and receive Your freedom in Christ. Amen!

Chapter Six

"It is better to dwell in the wilderness, than with a contentious and an angry woman." (Proverbs 21:19, KJV)

Can Wonder Woman Be Hormonal and Still Save the Day?

One Sunday night after a prayer service, I approached several sisters and asked them if they could pitch in with a food plate for a special upcoming church gathering. They all responded positively, except for one particular lady. I'm going to call her Helga. She was a middle-aged woman. I had heard her share with some other ladies that she was experiencing menopause. At that point in time, I didn't know much about menopause and unbalanced hormones and how they truly affected women. All I knew was that women with menopause and PMS tended to get moody. Helga was the type of person I had to be very careful with, regarding how I spoke to her. I sort of had to tip toe around her. That night I gently approached her and asked the following, "Hello Sister Helga. How are you doing?" She said, "I'm fine thank you, what can I do for you?" I thought to myself, "So far, so good, I'm not getting yelled at." I was singing victory too soon. With a big smile on my face, I asked her, "Sister Helga, all the sisters and I are bringing a plate for the gathering. Would you like to bring something?" She asked, "What do you want?" I said, "Is it possible that you can bring a very small bowl of guacamole?" She then replied with an outburst of anger, "How dare you ask me to bring such a thing! That plate is very hard to do and super expensive!" I then responded, "Ok, sister, don't worry about it." She then alleged, "Oh, now you want to prevent me from contributing?" I said, "No Sister Helga. You can bring anything you wish. The ladies just informed me that we are in need of a box of crackers. Would you like to bring one?" She answered hysterically, "Do you want to make me look like a fool in front of the other women who are bringing food? I will bring two boxes!"

By the grace of God, I safely and politely walked away. Later that night, I shared the incident with my husband and told him the following words, "I think that Helga's head is a little off. I can't believe she made a big deal out of the guacamole plate. She almost made guacamole out of me!" My husband replied, "You need to have patience with her. Maybe she had a bad day." I said, "I don't think so. She's always cranky!" He replied, "Well maybe she's just going through the change. You know, one day you might be going through that too." I regretfully replied, "I will never get menopause, and if I do, I will never act like Helga!" Later on, I learned that you should never say "Never!" During my twenties and thirties, I suffered from PMS with painful periods, but that did not stop me from being a multitasker, a go getter, and a somewhat gentler person. If I got cranky during my period, I would keep my distance as much as possible from the people at church or my friends, in order to not offend them. After the end of my cycle, I would bounce back with a clear mind. I felt happy, energetic, vibrant, and eager to meet any challenges without any fear.

However, as I was getting closer to my forties, I was unaware that perimenopause was creeping in, which caused even greater physical and emotional changes to my body. I began to feel more physically exhausted all the time and did not have the same energy that I was used to having; I also suffered from brain fog, which often made me forgetful. Emotionally, I would get overly sensitive, and sometimes I'd cry for no good reason. Little tasks felt like a mountain, which caused me to feel overwhelmed and anxious; more so, many times I felt irritable with no patience to deal with the kids and husband at home. All these symptoms would linger on for days. I often asked myself, "What happened to this beauty, had I turned into a beast?"

One Saturday afternoon, my husband and I were getting ready to go to a Bible school graduation service in which he was the director. I was very exhausted and at first I refused to attend the service, but my husband urged me to go. He was in charge of overseeing the program and had asked me to help him out with it. In addition, I was scheduled to sing a special graduation song. In the past, it was no trouble for me to do all this; however, now things were different. My body was not operating as it used to. All these symptoms that I mentioned above were interrupting me from performing my normal duties. As my husband explained the program to me, all of a sudden I became frantic and paranoid to the point that my nerves took over me. I remembered crying and yelling at him hysterically in the car, while driving toward the church. I was acting like a child who was throwing a tantrum, exclaiming to him, "I can't do this; I can't sing or perform in anything because, first of all, I do not remember the words to my song and secondly, I feel terribly drained. I refuse to help you, so please find someone else!"

When we got to the parking lot, he tried to calm me down. He said to me, "Honey, it's ok; I understand that you are not feeling well. When we get to the church lobby, I will try to find someone to help me with this task. All I want you to do is to go sit down, rest and be at peace." I was also not at my spiritual best that day, and I was not aware that the enemy was observing my neurotic behavior; he then decided to take advantage of the situation. When we walked into the church's lobby, there was a young girl who happened to be one of my husband's students from the Bible school. When he saw her, he politely asked for help and also asked her to escort me to the front row chairs where we were supposed to be seated. Shamefully, she began to flirt with him in my presence. She then grabbed my coat and purse, and threw them in a back seat far away from my husband's seat. Apparently, she did not want me to sit with him.

I was outraged and the first thing that came to my mind was the urge to grab this woman by her neck and whack her couple of times, but I could not find the courage to do that. I knew that it would not be Christ-like behavior; furthermore, I did not want to make a scene as the service commenced. My husband looked at my face and noticed that I was bothered by this woman's conduct. He immediately embraced me, scolded her and walked me to my seat. He said to me, "Honey, don't let the devil get the best of you and steal the blessing He has for you tonight. Know that I love you and only have eyes for you." I replied back, "I know you love me and you are right, but now, I need to get some air. I'm going to the ladies room." It's much harder for women than men to get over things like this so quickly. Men are practical, but women are very emotional. I still felt disturbed and irritated by the incident and acknowledged that I could not worship God in such a state; so I decided to run as fast as I could to a distant ladies room. I managed to tape an "Out of Service" sign to the door, so no one would bother me. My nerves felt out of control and my hands were shaking; I began to pray and ask God to intervene in my heart. After praying, I was looking at myself through the bathroom mirror, and told myself, "Evie, get a grip on yourself! You are not going to let this girl take over your role. Go out there and help your husband with what he asked you to do in the first place. Moreover, you will not give the devil the satisfaction of seeing you defeated, and no matter how you feel, you're going to sing, because it's for the Lord. You are God's wonder woman, and even though you might be a little hormonal, with His help, you can still save the day!" After praying and doing a small self-talk, I immediately felt His Spirit touch me and give me serenity. With a big smile on my face, I sat next to my husband and told him, "Honey, I'm ready to help you out and I'm going to sing." He looked at me and with a sigh of relief, he replied, "Honey, that's what I love about you; you always know how to bounce back."

After that incident, I began to suffer many other symptoms that made me think that perhaps I was going insane. I suspected that I was entering into perimenopause; but was not entirely sure. I visited various gynecologists and they all told me that I was too young to experience such thing. Also, they said that my symptoms were all psychological. They prescribed an anti-depressant and recommended that I see a psychiatrist, but I refused. I was not suffering from depression as an illness but rather feeling the blues from time to time. I knew that something was not working properly in my body but no one seemed to be giving me the right answers or correct treatment to ease my symptoms. A few years later, the Lord led me to a doctor who specialized in treating women with hormone imbalance, ovarian issues, and menopause. He performed many tests and was able to diagnose my health issues correctly. He confirmed my suspicions and to put me at ease, he said: "You are not crazy; you have now entered into perimenopause. Your ovaries are shrinking and they are not producing enough estrogen and the proper hormones your body needs; this is the reason for your emotional and physical symptoms." He then gave me the right treatment that I personally needed at that time. I applied His recommended treatment, and I saw a difference in me. My symptoms were gone and I felt normal again.

If you are a lively, godly woman just like me, who strives to live a happy life serving God, family, ministry, community, and/or career, but are experiencing symptoms of PMS, perimenopause, or a case of imbalance hormones; let me tell you, it does not mean that you are crazy, not spiritual enough, or demon possessed. This simply means that your body is going through changes and your hormones are going up and down like a rollercoaster. As your hormones fluctuate, you will experience various symptoms that can affect your normal daily living, but how can we deal with our hormonal symptoms and behavior?

Disclaimer

I would like to take this moment to deeply emphasize and make it clear, that because I am not a medical doctor or a gynecologist, I am not authorized to prescribe or recommend a proper medication, treatment or cure, in order to heal or alleviate the physical symptoms of PMS, perimenopause or menopause. There are many books and websites written by doctors that can help you to find ways to relieve the physical symptoms of hormonal imbalance, PMS and menopause. I recommend the following books: *"It's My Ovaries Stupid"* by Dr. Elizabeth Lee Vliet, and *"Hormone Revolution: Yes, You Can Naturally Restore & Balance Your Own Hormones,"* by Dr. Susan Lark. They cover all those female issues, and offer great recommendations on what to do in order to alleviate symptoms.

I also recommend that you as a woman care for your body. Do your regular checkups, and if you are suffering from harsh symptoms of PMS or perimenopause, seek a doctor that is willing to give you the proper treatments that will meet your own specific needs. When facing PMS, perimenopause or menopause, we will most likely feel symptoms of irritability, anxiety, be overly sensitive, experience crying spells and many other symptoms that affect our emotions. Doctors say that these symptoms are produced by shifting hormones and lack of estrogen in our ovaries. As Christian women, how are we supposed to act when our hormones go haywire? I would like to share some spiritual insights regarding what the Word of God prescribes to us on how to obtain the right attitude and how to deal with our emotions when being hormonal.

How Can We Ease the Emotional Aspect of PMS?

One Sunday morning after our church service ended, everyone was greeting each other at the lobby. While I was walking through the crowd, I noticed a young woman sitting in a corner. She didn't look too happy. I also observed how people tried to avoid any contact with her. I asked my friend Angie, "What's wrong with Shanika and what's with the angry face?" Angie responded, "Oh, she's kind of moody today. She just snapped at Kendra and some other people. I approached her and asked her what was wrong, and she told me that she wasn't in the mood to talk to people. She wanted to be left alone. I guess she has PMS today, which means she is being a PRETTY MEAN SISTER!"

We have heard many jokes and definitions of women with PMS but frankly, for those who are suffering from it, it is very hard to laugh along. When it hits, it can make us feel unhappy. Dr. Melissa Conrad Stoppler defines PMS as follows: "Premenstrual syndrome (known as PMS) involves a variety of physical, mental, and behavioral symptoms tied to a woman's menstrual cycle. By definition, symptoms occur during the two weeks before a woman's period starts, known as the luteal phase of the menstrual cycle."[38] Premenstrual syndrome can cause various physical symptoms and it can also throw us into an emotional spin wheel, leaving us feeling irritable and experiencing the blues.

Doctors recommend special drugs or medicine for depression and counseling in order to relieve the extreme emotional conditions of PMS. If you have a physical and psychological disorder, I strongly recommend that you consult with your physician for treatment. However, as a minister of Christ, I will share my own personal experiences and recommendations that have worked for me when dealing with the emotional side of PMS. During the times when my turbulent hormones try to tear my spirit apart, I take refuge in prayer and in God's Word. This helps me cope with my emotional symptoms and tame the beast within me, as I like to call it. Relying on prayer and on God's Word will produce calmness and peace in our souls as we face emotional symptoms. If you are going through something similar, allow me to encourage you to do the following things that can also help you in such a time:

Meditate in God's Word & Pray.

Whenever those stormy hormones cause you to feel sad, depressed, anxious, or nervous, and may overwhelm you as you deal with the normal stress of life, stop for a moment, meditate, and rely on God's Word. Reflect on the good things that the Lord has given you. Consider the peace that He constantly offers you through His Word. His Word brings comfort and serenity to the soul, and also promises healing for your mind, body, and inner being. Premenstrual syndrome and a case of imbalanced hormones can sometimes leave us feeling emotionally drained and spiritually exhausted. It is a time where we might be feeling like we are walking through a dark and lonely path. If you're feeling that way, take heart my friend. There's always a light at the end of the tunnel.

God promises that as you place your trust in Him, He will lead you to green pastures where your mind, body and soul will receive complete rest (Ps. 23:2-4). The apostle Paul also encourages us to *pray continuously* (1 Thes. 5:17). Let us pray even when we don't feel like doing so. It is important to set a time alone to pray. We can also pray in our minds and in our inner being at any time of the day. God will always listen; even the smallest whispers of your heart are music to His ears. Prayer moves the hand of the Lord in our favor and it brings us closer to Him. Prayer also brings changes and can move the mountains in our lives; so PRAY at all times and pray in the Spirit.

The apostle Paul tells us that the Holy Spirit intercedes for us in our weaknesses (Rom. 8:26). When we are feeling the heavy symptoms of PMS or hormonal imbalance, our minds can get foggy and we cannot think straight. Sometimes we do not understand what we must pray for. We are encouraged to pray in the Spirit in every circumstance **(Eph. 6:18)**. As we pray in the Spirit, the Holy Spirit pleads to our heavenly Father for our most intimate and profound needs, thoughts and the things that we do not dare speak about, which only God knows. Let us pray in the Spirit, especially when we suffer from the effects of PMS or imbalanced hormones. The Holy Spirit is on our side and understands our deepest feelings.

Speak God's Word to Yourself and Breathe

People can experience anxiety for all kinds of reasons. Anxiety can also be a symptom produced by PMS or imbalanced hormones. A great way to deal with anxiety is to cast our cares to God. When we feel oppressed by anxiety due to hormones that can rob us of rest and steal away our breath, God's Word tells us to "...banish anxiety from your heart and cast off the troubles of your body,..." (Eccles. 11:10). One day, as I was flying back from visiting my dad in Nevada, I was overcome with anxiety. Getting an anxiety attack while being inside of a plane is not a pretty picture. It was a late evening flight and as we ascended, the flight attendant dimmed the cabin lights so that people could get some shuteye. I remember feeling a sense of panic as I felt the cabin getting darker and darker. I knew that my shifting hormones were causing this anxiety, because I had never had an anxiety attack inside a plane. All of sudden my heart started palpitating very fast and I began to feel shortness of breath. To make matters worse, I was flying alone without my husband, who is always able to comfort me. In my mind, I wanted to scream, "Someone, please, get me out of this plane!" At that moment, I thought to myself, "That can't be possible; we are thousands of miles up in the air and there is nothing that anyone can do to help me get out of this plane." I then remembered two things that would take away the anxiety I was experiencing.

First, I began to speak God's Word to myself. His Word empowered me to overcome the anxiety and it began to quiet my soul. Second, I put into practice what my husband has always told me whenever I experienced anxiety. He'd say, "Breathe! Honey, take a deep breath, inhale, and slowly exhale three times and you will feel better." My husband had explained to me that when we enter into a state of panic, there is not enough oxygen going into the brain and we cannot think clearly. Speaking His Word to myself and taking a few deep breaths allowed me to feel a whole lot better. God's Word and breathing properly can reduce tension, anxiety, and stress. It also produces relaxation by clearing our minds and bringing relief to our emotional state of being. When we totally get a hold of His Word and of the oxygen that He has given us, it can benefit our minds, souls and bodies. If ever comes a moment that you feel any kind of anxiety, all you have to do is *speak God's Word to yourself and breathe!*

How Can We Ease the Emotional Aspect of Perimenopause?

What is perimenopause? Dr. Shannon K. Laughlin-Tommaso from the Mayo Clinic defines perimenopause as follows: "Perimenopause means 'around menopause' and refers to the time period during which a woman's body makes its natural transition toward permanent infertility (menopause)."[39] This means that when a woman reaches perimenopause, her menstrual cycle will become irregular to the point that it will be gone, and it is possible that she will no longer be able to get pregnant. Perimenopause leads you into menopause, and its emotional symptoms are mostly the same.

Women with perimenopause will experience various physical and emotional symptoms like anxiety, panic attacks, insomnia, body aches, exhaustion, depression, irritability and many more symptoms.

The emotional symptoms of perimenopause can sometimes make you feel as if you might be going crazy. You can also feel that you are not yourself anymore, or that a monster has invaded your body. I know it sounds quite dramatic, but Dr. Vliet confirms what I have just said concerning women that have entered into perimenopause. She says, "Other symptoms develop or become magnified-you may feel an alien has taken over your body."[40] Some women suffer different symptoms, while others feel their symptoms in a severe manner. If you are suffering from perimenopause, it is highly recommended to reduce stress as much as possible.

Stress can trigger your symptoms to get worse. There have been cases of premenopausal women that have abandoned their husbands or families, have suffered from strokes or have developed other health issues due to terrible stress with their careers, work, or family. These are women who are facing terrible stress in either caring for their elderly parents, dealing with difficult teenagers at home, a problematic marriage, or other stressful life events. The shifting hormones can affect not just our physical bodies, but also our emotional being. Our emotions can get wired up.

There are some premenopausal women that become emotional eaters or emotional buyers when their hormones are out of control. When feeling hormonal, it is best to focus on something positive and useful that will benefit us. If we become emotional buyers when facing perimenopause, we're not able to think clearly and so, I recommend going window shopping and leaving the wallet at home, so that you will not be tempted to overspend. Other women use food to alleviate their uncontrolled emotions. If you are an emotional eater, I recommend that you focus on a healthy hobby that you enjoy. In doing so, it can take your mind off of food. Whether we are facing hormonal imbalance, PMS, perimenopause or menopause, we will also feel at times short-tempered. When feeling irritable, I have to say that it does not give us a license to be rude or to hurt people with outbursts of anger. It's so easy to offend when we are angry. The Holy Spirit has convicted me many times concerning how to treat people when I feel irritable.

I have learned that whenever we face moments of irritability, we ought to do the following: If dealing with a difficult person at your job that gets on your nerves or other people for that matter, it is best to greet kindly, gently walk away, keep a distance, or simply stay silent. In doing so, we'll keep ourselves from saying something foolish that we will later regret. Let us take King Solomon's advice. He says, "When words are many, transgression is not lacking, but whoever restrains his lips is prudent" (Prov. 10:19, ESV). I think he meant that particular bible verse for us hormonal women, who get irritable often. If anybody knew women and their hormonal changes very well, I'd say it was King Solomon. Some might wonder why he had so many women in his life. Perhaps he could not get enough of them, had a sex addiction, or was trying to find the perfect woman. The Bible clearly states that he loved and had a taste for many foreign women. It also says that he had seven hundred wives and three hundred concubines (1 Kings 11:1, 3).

I don't know if this man ever got any sleep, but I do know that Solomon realized that he preferred to live in a tiny space somewhere in the rooftop of his home, than to live with an irritating and nagging wife (Prov. 21:9). When we get hormonal, we tend to nag and not in the good way. That is a fact, and since King Solomon lived with so many women, it is obvious that he figured that out. The Bible says that Solomon compares a quarrelsome wife to a rainy day (Prov. 27:15-16). By this, I think that he meant that if one has a rainy day, it can rain all day long, and if a husband has a wife with hormonal issues, she most likely will nag all day long without stopping. There are other ways to help ourselves, when feeling irritable due to our shifting hormones. One thing I used to practice when I had a period (and I recommend this particular habit to women during their fertile years) was to track periods down by keeping a calendar. When my kids were younger, I use to pin a big monthly calendar on the fridge door. On the week before my period, I would jot down in big words, "Beware people, the angry monster is about to come out on this particular week!" I made sure my kids and husband would thoroughly read the calendar, so that they would be on high alert! They knew that they had to be super nice and accommodating during that specific time, and I would put myself into heavy prayer for God's strength and serenity.

Honestly, I have to say, that things didn't always go as I hoped, but at least my family was warned as to why I lacked patience and got irritable. I also tried as much as possible to hold my tongue when getting easily irritated, so that I would not hurt their feelings. If I did, I quickly apologized. In doing so, my kids would understand that I'm only human and that I'm living in an imperfect body. It is important to know that if we offend because of hormonal issues or other reasons, we must ask for forgiveness. In addition, I had to learn to submit my body to the Lord by allowing Him to be in control of my hormones and not permit them to be the boss of me. It is very hard to control our emotions when we have unbalanced hormones. It feels like your body and mind is living in chaos and no one understands, however, it is *not* impossible to be self-controlled.

We can receive internal calmness when we yield those shifting hormones to our heavenly Father, thus through Him our emotions can be at ease. The Bible tells us to let our lives be led by God's Spirit and not by our flesh (Rom. 8:13). Our earthly flesh will cause us to say and do things that are not appropriate and that are ungodly. However, if we allow the Holy Spirit to take control of our whole being, we will live in true freedom and not be slaves to our emotions and our bodies. This endeavor can be accomplished mainly by submitting ourselves and unbalanced hormones on a daily basis to the Lord. As God's true wonder women, we can be humanly hormonal and still save the day through His divine power.

Biblical Women with Hormonal Issues

Women with hormonal issues have existed since the beginning of time. Right after Eve's fallout, woman's bodies began to feel the effect of a fallen nature. Let us examine the attitudes of two particular godly women of the Bible times, who were as human as you and I are. Just like us, they too experienced a menstrual cycle and the same distress of the effects of unbalanced hormones. We will observe how they handled themselves in the midst of their daily activities.

Martha

Martha was considered to be the housekeeper, or the person in charge of the household. She had two siblings, Lazarus and Mary. As the housekeeper, she must have had many responsibilities in keeping the affairs of the home, and she made sure that it all ran smoothly. That alone can be stressful. Many people jump right into judging Martha for her whining and complaining, as recorded in (Lk. 10:40). I do not excuse her actions, because even Jesus reprimanded her. However, as a woman, I understand the human side of her. She had her flaws, was a normal woman like any other, and probably had hormonal issues, but we also know that she loved the Lord.

If you are wondering what triggered this woman to complain on the day that Jesus visited, we must first see the whole picture. Some theologians suggest that she was not spiritual enough because of her approach toward Jesus. I do agree that in this case she blew the opportunity to receive a blessing, but I also believe that as a woman, her hormones must have had something to do with her attitude. I'm not saying that all the sins and wrong actions that we commit are caused mainly by our hormones. Jesus said that sin starts in the heart, "For out of the heart come evil thoughts, murder, adultery, sexual immorality, theft, false testimony, slander" (Matt. 15:19). We must take in consideration, that if we happened to feel and have an irritable moment due to a case of unbalanced hormones, it can affect our judgment and thinking. It is then that we should strive to depend on God's grace.

Let us analyze the situation. Jesus decides to pay his beloved friends a visit (Lk. 10:38). He really loved this family. I'm thinking that on that particular day, even though the Bible does not say that Martha was menstruating or give us details as to why she acted the way she did when Jesus came to visit, I imagine that she must have been in the verge or approaching her menstrual cycle. This leads me to believe that she could have been suffering from PMS and that could have been a factor for her behavior. I mean, think about it, if you were Martha and you were close to getting your period, you're probably going to be hormonal. The hormones begin to fluctuate a week or days prior to the actual periods, producing various symptoms, especially irritability. More so, if you were expecting Jesus, God himself in the flesh, to visit your home and you notice that the house is messy, your siblings are not cooperating with you, and dinner isn't ready yet; that alone would definitely stress you out. No woman likes to receive company in those conditions.

Let us *imagine* this scenario. That day Martha probably had a million things to do; she was most likely multitasking. It's late, the fish is still cooking and the table isn't set. Martha is running like a chicken without a head trying to set the table while tidying the place as fast as possible. At this time, Jesus is knocking at the door and Martha probably hollers at her sister, "Mary, get the door!" Her heart is vastly palpitating. In that moment, her stress level is over the roof and her hormones are going haywire. As soon as Jesus comes in, Mary attends to her guest. The irritated Martha sees Mary and thinks to herself, "I still have to finish up this dinner, I'm running late getting everything done and Mary is just plain lazy!" At this point, Martha's brain is foggy and cannot understand and comprehend that her Lord and Savior is sitting in her living room, waiting to have a moment to chat with her. Instead of her rejoicing that her Master had come to visit, she allowed her hormones to take control and began to whine and complain to Jesus with an irritable tone. Martha acted as a typical hormonal woman who had a PMS moment. Did this mean that she did not love the Lord? John describes her as a person who had acknowledged and had faith that Jesus is the Son of God who had come into the world (Jn. 11:27). Also, as explained in the book of John, Martha was serving the tables at a special dinner party for Jesus (12:2). In this passage, the

Bible does not mention of any exasperation on the part of Martha. At this particular moment, she was probably over her cycle and the tempest of her fluctuating hormones is resting like a tranquil sea. This time she is not irritated, yelling and complaining. She is serving the Lord most likely happy and with a servant's heart.

Mary (Martha's Sister)

Mary, on the other hand, as a woman who also had a period every month knew how to submit her hormones at the feet of Jesus. She too must have faced trials, sickness and hardships, but every time that she had a chance to hear her Lord speak, she would take advantage of those moments. She knew that when hearing her master's voice, she would receive knowledge and healing. Let us model after this woman who knew how to surrender her hormones and her entire being to Jesus. In doing so, we can receive His touch of healing when facing the effects of shifting hormones.

The Woman with the Issue of Blood

Our Lord and Creator understand our human nature and our weaknesses. He knows everything about us and recognizes how fragile we can be; therefore, He has a special compassion over us. The book of Luke recounts a story of Christ's compassion over a woman who had been suffering from a hemorrhage (8:43-48). She had endured this illness for twelve years. Since a menstrual cycle was considered to be something dirty, being that she had been discharging blood for so long, people viewed her as an unclean woman. She was most likely treated as an outcast from society (Lev.

15:19-30). When she heard that Jesus was in town, she rushed over to see Him. As she was faced with a multitude of people, it made it difficult to get to Him, but in her faith and determination, she pressed through and touched the hem of His garment. Instantly, Christ's power was drawn from Him and she was able to receive her healing.

When Jesus asked who touched Him, she came forward. Because of her unwanted condition, she was not supposed to be in a public setting where she would touch anyone. I can imagine her feeling scared, thinking that Jesus was going to scold her and point his finger at her. On the contrary, He embraced her by calling her daughter. He gave her peace and the healing that she had longed for. Today He also calls us His daughters, and He is willing to heal our hurting bodies and help us through when suffering from the effects of tempestuous hormones. All we need to do is to reach out with all of our faith, and we will receive a touch of the Master's love.

Conclusion

There are times in our lives when we have thought that being a woman in itself is a challenge, but let me say this: The greater the trials we encounter in our own bodies, and the greater the hardships we have to endure; the greater the rewards are if we allow God to fully take control of our whole being. When dealing with hormonal imbalance, PMS, perimenopause or menopause, we can experience His glory in every physical and emotional phase we go through. Allow me to finish this chapter by responding to the question: Can Wonder Woman be hormonal and still save the day? It has been my experience that as God's true wonder woman and as a human being, I too have suffered symptoms from hormonal imbalances. Nonetheless, through His infinite strength and His Spirit that dwells inside of me, I have been empowered to overcome all kinds of hardships. The answer would be yes; God's true wonder women can be hormonal and still save the day, through His mighty power that helps us in all our circumstances. His strength is perfect in us, each and every day (2 Cor. 12:9).

Prayer for Healing

Dear Heavenly Father, I come to You with complete humility, recognizing that I am simply a human being living in an imperfect body; striving to seek a perfect God. I ask You to please bring healing to my mind, body, and soul. Please take full control of my fluctuating hormones that want to shift my emotions like a roller coaster without an end.

In this very moment, allow me to experience the touch of Your healing hands over my bodily internal organs. May Your Spirit bring me complete peace and quiet my soul within me as I experience the effects and symptoms of shifting hormones that work to obstruct the quality of life that You wish me to enjoy. I know that in You I can be made whole, and that through Your infinite grace, I can be strengthened and empowered. Thank You my Lord, for caring for me and for understanding me when I do not feel good. In Jesus name, I pray. Amen.

Chapter Seven

"I also want the women to dress modestly, with decency and propriety..." (1 Timothy 2:9)

God's True Wonder Woman Fashion

A certain preacher was invited to minister at a women's convention. I wasn't able to go to that particular event, but a friend of mine attended it. She told me that the speaker was dynamic and had a powerful message. The first night, as he preached God's Word, the women were blessed. When he finished preaching, he made an altar call. Many went to the altar for prayer. As he began to pray over them, there were some women who started to jump for joy because they were receiving God's touch and deliverance. The following night, my friend noticed that something was different at the altar call. As the women were standing, many were covered with a big piece of cloth over their chest and legs. I asked her why they did this. She replied, "Evie, last night when the preacher was praying for these ladies, somehow they were dressed too provocative and sexy. Some women wore extremely short skirts and were bearing a lot of skin. Others were very voluptuous wearing low-cut blouses and showing a lot of cleavage. When they were receiving blessings, as they were jumping for joy, their breasts were all over the place [what my friend meant was that their chest was overexposed]! The preacher was having a hard time concentrating and felt uncomfortable. He demanded that the women would be covered."

One would think, *if this preacher was a godly man, why would he be bothered by these women's appearance? He is supposed to be focusing on ministering to them and not be distracted by their attire. Women have the right to wear whatever they want, and to wear it however they please. The preacher has no business getting distracted by their apparel.* I am not defending the preacher but I can understand where he's coming from. Let us comprehend how differently men and women are sexually aroused. We are created with five human senses: vision, hearing, taste, smell, and touch.

Most women are sexually aroused not by vision, but mostly, we are aroused by the sense of touch. It takes more than a look, smell, taste, or sound to get a woman stimulated. A tender touch on her hands or a warm embrace can light up a sparkle within her senses. A husband can gently caress his wife, but if he wants to get some sexual intimacy before the night is over, he'll be smart enough to give that woman not just a romantic, candlelit dinner, but also a shoulder rub, backrub, or even a body massage. Sure enough, she will respond.

On the other hand, men are sexually aroused by the sense of sight. It doesn't matter what name or position a man may have or how spiritual he is, a man will always be a man. If a provocatively dressed woman walks by them, some men will be verbal in expressing their excitement and others will be reserved, but still their eyes will turn to look. It is in their nature. One night, as I was watching an award show on TV, two celebrities, male and female, came forward to present an award. The female celebrity was dressed beautifully but she had a very low cut dress, and was not leaving much room to the imagination. After the show was over, the male celebrity was criticized because he made a comment about this woman's breasts. Instead of reading his line that was written for him in the teleprompter, he was too focused on this woman's grand cleavage. I noticed that this female celebrity was not too pleased with his comment. If I had a chance to say something, I would tell her, "Listen Missy, if you do not want men to focus on your breasts, why expose them?" I know there are worldly men out there who are filled with lust, and whether a woman is covered or not, they will stare at her chest. Why provoke even more by wearing indecent attire? Christian women can dress beautifully and become fashionistas if they wish without flaunting their sensuality.

It is not my intention to tell you what to wear and make judgment in a legalistic form; but rather to bring you up to date on the wrongful message portrayed by celebrities in the entertainment world concerning fashion morality and how a woman ought to dress. Whether they acknowledge it or not, fashion designers, celebrities, and pop culture in general have a great influence on young people and women today. They set the fashion trends because they are admired, and women tend to copy their styles. The world's message regarding fashion to this generation of women is, "if you have it, flaunt it!" and, "wearing clothes that show skin is acceptable, and to cover up is a thing of the past."

The Word of God clearly tells us, "Do not conform any longer to the pattern of this world,..." (Rom. 12:2). What does this mean? My personal observation of what the apostle Paul is trying to tell us is to be careful not to imitate worldly styles, designs, customs, and behaviors that will not honor God. As Christian women, whose message are we going to follow? My purpose in this chapter is for us to learn what the Word of God tells us as to how He would like us to dress that will make us look and feel beautiful in His eyes. We will discuss three recommendations given by the apostle Paul on how a Christian woman, married or single, ought to dress in order to bring Him glory. I would like to also convey to all of the beautiful women of God that it is okay to love fashion and clothes as long as we wear them in a decent manner.

Biblical Background on Fashion

What is fashion? The Encarta Dictionary defines *fashion* as "a style." Fashion has to do with trends, different looks, and fabrics, as well as dress styles, clothes, jewelry, and hairdos. Today's fashion industry presents many different dress styles that can be very appealing. Most women spend thousands of dollars each year on clothing and shoes, and love to dress in the latest styles. Although the fashion industry of this modern world constantly comes up with diverse styles of clothing every year, I have to say that they cannot take credit for being the ones to invent clothes and fashion. Clothes and fashion have existed since the beginning of time.

God was the very first fashion designer to create the original garments introduced to the world. Before sin entered our realm, life was supposed to be much simpler and without the kind of worries that most women have every morning when they ask themselves, "What am I going to wear today?" I don't know about you, but I have to confess, that like any normal woman that loves clothes and shoes, when opening my closet door, frustration and anxiety hit me from time to time as I decide what to wear to go to work, church, or any upcoming event. We usually use this expression, "I don't have anything to wear," when in reality, for the most part, our closets are overloaded with clothes. Nowadays, we have so many options and a variety of outfits to wear that it can be mindboggling.

Man and woman's wardrobe back in the Garden of Eden was simple and without any hassles. They were meant to walk around in their birthday suits and live happily ever after without any fashion dilemmas. The Bible says, "Adam and Eve strolled naked through the garden without any shame" (Gen. 2:25). This leads me to believe that this was the Lord's ultimate fashion for this couple in this divine place. Their nakedness was covered by God's glory. He dressed their bodies in a special garment made out of holiness and pure innocence. I agree with Spence-Jones in his book, *The Pulpit Commentary: Genesis* as he further explains why Adam and Eve, while naked, felt no shame:

> "The first pair of human beings are henceforth recognized in their relationship to one another as husband

and wife. And they were not ashamed. Not because they were wholly uncultivated and their moral insight undeveloped (Knobel, Kalisch), but because their souls were arrayed in purity, and 'their bodies were made holy, through the spirit which animated them' (Keil). 'They were naked, but yet they were not so. Their bodies were the clothing of their internal glory; and their internal glory was the clothing of their nakedness' (Delitzsch)".[41]

Let us learn how Adam and Eve's godly fashion suffered a transition and how it affected our world's fashion today.

The Cause for a Transition

What changed? What was the cause for the transition from our original fashion? After Adam and Eve sinned by eating the forbidden fruit, their consciences were awakened to realize that they were naked, and sin had taken away their God-given innocence and purity (Gen. 3:6-7). God's glory and communion departed from them. They found themselves in a state of shame and in need for covering their bodies. Before sin came, Adam and Eve were not aware that clothes existed, and also had never worn any physical attire in the Garden of Eden. When sin opened their eyes, they were embarrassed by their condition, and the first thing they took ahold of to cover up was some fig leaves, with which they hemmed themselves (Gen. 3:7).

The Lord is not only the Creator of all things, but He is also a great fashion designer. After He questioned and sentenced this offending couple for their sin (although the Bible doesn't say this specifically) I imagined Him looking straight at them and thinking to himself: *These people not only blew it big time, but what were they thinking by putting on some pile of leaves to cover up? This will not do. It seems they have a wardrobe malfunction going on here. That's no way for my children to leave the Garden. I'm going to design some clothes for them.*

In spite of their sin, we saw God's mercy, love, and provision over them (Gen. 3:21). He made sure that they would not leave His holy place in ill fitted rags; but rather, that they would leave in an updated fashion, wearing comfortable clothes to cover up their shame and also to protect them from their new hostile environment. The very first fur coats were invented by God. J.P. Lang and others in their commentary on the Scriptures affirm that these garments were made out of animal skin for a specific purpose: as a symbol of God's grace:

> "This clothing would appear to be a sacramental sign of grace, a type of the death of Christ, and of the being clothed with the holy righteousness of the God-man. Keil disputes this, although firmly maintaining that in this act of God there was laid the ground of the sacrificial offering of beasts."[42]

God sacrificed animals to clothe his creation as a symbol of how Christ would be sacrificed for us, that our shame may be covered by his blood. However, today we no longer have the need to sacrifice animals to cover our transgression. Christ, the Lamb of God, died so that we would receive redemption. Therefore, the need for animal sacrifices is eliminated; and we are forever clothed in his grace (Jn. 1:29). The main cause for a transition in fashion was produced by sin and initiated at the Garden of Eden when the first humans, our forefathers, were expelled from it.

After the fall, nudity was not accepted because sin had torn away its purity. Throughout the Bible, nudity exemplifies the spiritual condition of His people. The Lord declared to His people that their nakedness would be uncovered as a sign that their sin would be exposed and because of it, it would lead them into slavery **(Isa. 47:3)**. The Lord's purpose for clothing was first of all to cover our nudity; second, to protect us from harsh weather; and third, His intentions for our clothing were that they be worn in a way that would keep us from lustful passions. Our clothing was not meant to be utilized or worn to show our sensuality.

Now that clothes were invented, they were to be used in a holy, decent and beautiful manner that would represent His glory in us (Ezek. 16:10-14). However, sin had affected the original holy plans for clothes and fashion. It corrupted the minds of people, especially those of foreign nations to invent extravagant clothing. Their certain styles of clothing were dedicated to their pagan gods and were also utilized with the purpose of displaying pride, vanity, and cause lustful desires. God had told the Israelites to keep their clothing simple and pure (Deut. 22:11, Lev. 19:19), but the Israelites began to copy the pagans' styles of clothing and the Lord was not very happy about it. The Bible recounts that God brought judgment upon those who adapted foreign clothing (Zeph. 1:8). Bently, in his book, *Opening up Zephaniah,* explains what motivated the people of Judea to adapt worldly styles of clothing. He says: "This would seem to indicate that the ordinary, simple clothing of God's people had been considered to be too dowdy by some of the Judeans, so they copied the fashions and styles of dress of the nations around them. They should have learned that imitating heathen people and their practices can only lead to catastrophe."[43]

The Lord is not against us wearing beautiful clothing and accessories, but when we wear them with the wrong motives in our hearts or wear indecent apparel, we are not glorifying Him, and His beauty in us is hindered. If God blesses us with a fine-looking dress to wear, then let us wear it in a godly fashion with a humble and Christ-like attitude. As Christian women, it is important for us to learn what kinds of clothes and styles we should wear that not only beautify us physically, but more importantly bring glory to Him, especially when attending church.

Fashion in the Old Testament

The kings in the Old Testament wore special robes that represented their calling and occupation. The Bible described how David dressed when he danced before the Lord (2 Sam. 6:14). The following are some scriptures that describe the main outward apparel and fashion of the Christians of the Bible (1 Sam. 2:18, Jn. 19:23 and Isa. 20:2). For the most part, people wore robes, tunics, sackcloth, and sandals. There was a special priestly garment ordered by God to be made for Aaron and his sons. These garments were intended, first of all, to be worn exclusively while the priest entered into the Holy place, offered his worship and ministered. They were also intended to give His priests dignity and honor. The garments were composed of "a breast piece, an ephod, a robe, a woven tunic, a turban, and a sash." (Exod. 28:2-43).

Worshippers' Attire

The priests who were in charge of worshipping at the altar were carefully instructed by Moses on how to approach God when worshipping. They had to be discreet concerning their attire. They were not allowed to wear any clothes that were see-through or that exposed intimate parts of the body. The Lord told them: "And do not go up to my altar on steps, or your private parts may be exposed" (Exod. 20:26). It seemed that their clothes, according to C. F. Pfeiffer were loose. He says, "Flowing garments would be lifted by the raised foot and the body would thus be disclosed."[44] It appeared that they did not wear undergarments and when going up the stairs to the altar, their private parts were visible. This action offended God and it also caused a distraction to those who were attending the worship service. It was likely that during those early years of the Bible times, people did not wear underclothes. The Lord gave instructions to Moses to have his most skilled tailors make Aaron and his priests' undergarments that would cover up their private parts. He said, "Make linen undergarments as a covering for the body, reaching from the waist to the thigh" (Exod. 28:42). It was expected for the priests and Levites to be completely covered up when they entered the temple for worshipping.

Modern Priests and Levites

The undergarment situation back in Moses' time certainly does not apply to us because naturally we all wear undergarments when attending church; however, in our modern times, there are other challenges pertaining to how people dress when worshipping. Let us not ignore that there are some churchgoers who have adapted worldly clothing styles and have brought them into our churches. The Lord cares about how we dress when attending worship service. He wants us to understand that although styles of clothing continue to evolve, God's principles remain the same. One of the reasons that I added this particular chapter to this book was because not a lot of people talk about the need to address the issue of appropriate attire for Christian woman, worship leaders, and worship teams when attending church. On a particular Sunday morning as I was ministering at a church in California, a pastor's wife approached me and asked, "Pastor Evie, can you please give me some advice on how to speak to the women in my church, especially the worship singers? They dress inappropriate with sensual clothing. People get distracted and the men are too busy lusting over them. This situation is becoming a problem in my church."

God is not pleased when we attend church wearing clothing that makes us look sensual. This directs the attention to us and it takes the focus off Him. Furthermore, it provokes men to lust after us. The same principles stated in 1Timothy 2:9 are especially to be applied to women in the worship team and worship leaders. Whether we realize it or not, we are role models to others. The apostle Peter reminds us that we are God's chosen generation and royal priesthood

(1 Pet. 2:9). We have been chosen to be His modern priestesses and Levites, and if we lead worship, let us do it dressed in a most respectable fashion. It is His desire that the clothing we choose to wear will be pleasing to Him and also give us dignity and honor. If you are a worship leader, member of the worship team, a minister, or just attend church, I would like to offer some small tips concerning how to wear certain clothing in a more decent manner. When wearing v-neck shirts and low cut blouses, it is recommended to wear a camisole or a mock camisole such as a Cami Secret (a piece of cloth that can be attached to your bra under your shirt). This allows coverage over your cleavage. If you happen to be a chesty woman, it is recommended not to wear very tight blouses. They accentuate your figure and the focus will no longer be on the Lord, but on you. There are ways to cover up by utilizing pretty jackets or wearing loose blouses.

I reiterate that we do not have to give up fashionable clothing. We can look fabulous without compromising our standards regarding godly apparel. Just as God admonished his priests in the Old Testament to take careful consideration on how they dressed while offering their worship at the altar, we are also cautioned to do the same because what we wear matters to God, and it also affects the people around us.

Fashion in the New Testament

Back in the New Testament, the church of Ephesus faced issues that are similar to those that our contemporary church is facing today concerning fashion. The city of Ephesus was a pagan city filled with lust and promiscuity. It was also commercially rich and probably a city where enticing fashions predominated. The Christian women began to imitate and apply a worldly fashion and conduct carrying it into the worship service. This created problems in the church. The apostle Paul realized that these particular issues concerning women's apparel in the church needed to be addressed. He says, "I also want the women to dress modestly, with decency and propriety, adorning themselves not with elaborate hairstyles or gold or pearls or expensive clothes, but with good deeds, appropriate for women who profess to worship God" (1 Tim. 2:9-10). Was he against that the women come to church dress nicely with fashionable clothing and adornments?

As the apostle Paul visited the church of Ephesus, he made a fashion intervention. He reminded Timothy to encourage the women to be careful in their conduct and how they ought to dress as they offer their worship unto God when coming to church. He advised that the women prioritize caring for their inner being, which should be composed of a holy attitude of the heart, more than their outward appearance. However, he did not prohibit the women from adorning themselves with beautiful fine clothing. Rather, he was referring to the *excessive* use of accessories and also to indecent attire that could lead to pride, vanity and lustful desires. The book, *"A Commentary on the Holy Scriptures: 1 & 2 Timothy,"* explains what the apostle Paul meant in this passage regarding appropriate apparel when attending church.

> "The object of the Apostle is not to enjoin a general rule of life for Christian women, but especially for their demeanor at the place of prayer. He does not forbid all ornament, but only the excess which is a

mark of frivolity and love of display, and awakens impure passions."[45]

Three Biblical Principals

There are three biblical principles recommended by the apostle Paul to be applied unto the Christian women's dress code. He recommends that women should dress *modestly*, with *decency* and *propriety*. We will focus on these three principles, which will serve as a guideline. It can help us to learn and discern in what ways God would want us to dress and understand why we should not follow certain worldly fashions and trends that are not appropriate when attending church. God is a God of order and he also loves great fashion. If we dress applying these principles stated in the Scriptures, as His true wonder women we will walk in an orderly and holy style, clothed in God's true fashion.

Modestly

Modestly is the first word used by the apostle Paul in regards to women's attire (1 Tim. 2:9). In order to dress modestly, we must understand its definition and its roots. The root word for modestly comes from the Greek word, *Aidos,* which means "respect, reverence and regard for others"[46] Ephesus was a rich city and into fashions. In order for a woman to be accepted into society, she had to buy the most expensive jewelry, copy the latest hairdo, and follow its latest fashion trends. Women lived for fashion and carried the most extravagant apparel to show off.

One of the problems that the Christian women of the Ephesus church were having was that they'd dress for church with the wrong motives. Instead of concentrating on worshipping, their main focus was to flaunt their beauty and wealth as they competed with one another wearing the latest fashion in dress, hairstyle and accessories. The women were too concerned with their attire, and dressed to attract attention as if church was a fashion show. Attending the worship service was an event all about them and not about God. The apostle Paul encouraged the women to dress with aidos/modesty as a way of honoring the Lord with reverence, respect and regard for others. This meant that they were not to dress too flashy or wear accessories in an excessive fashion that would draw attention to themselves. Immodest dress also caused discord and envy, since there were also women in their midst who were poor and not financially able to keep up with such over-the-top fashion.

Others might also think that this means that we have to attend our worship services clothed in rags, and dreary clothes, and furthermore, dressed as if we live in a convent, in order to be seen as holy women. In their view, dressing in designer clothes or expensive clothes might be considered a sin or unacceptable to God. R. C. H. Lenski, in the book, *The interpretation of St. Paul's Epistles to the Colossians, to the Thessalonians, to Timothy, to Titus and to Philemon,* helps us to better understand what the apostle Paul is trying to tell us regarding dressing modestly:

"The fact that flashy jewelry would be displayed with costly ἱματισμός or "clothing" is apparent. Such a woman wants to make a stunning impression. Her mind is entirely on herself; she is unfit for worship. This verse does not refer merely to sex attraction. How many women who are past that age are given to the silly vanity of dress? Paul is not insisting on drab dress. Even this may be worn with vanity; the very drabness may be made a display. Each according to her station in life: the queen not being the same as her lady in waiting, the latter not the same as her noble mistress. Each with due propriety as modesty and propriety will indicate to her both when attending divine services and when appearing in public elsewhere."[47]

The principle of dressing modestly is to dress our best according to our financial means and with a Godly attitude. We must keep in mind that attending worship services should be all about God and not about us.

Decency

Let us briefly examine the second principle that is recommended by the apostle Paul concerning how women should dress. He also says "dress...with decency" (v. 9). The English Standard version reads, "respectable appearance" The Greek word for respectable is *Kosmios*.[48] It means honorable, modest, appropriate and decent. We are urged as Christian women to dress in an honorable manner with appropriate apparel as we attend church and elsewhere. We live in a culture where dressing your best for church is considered to be an old-fashioned thing. Dressing casually, without having any concern regarding appropriate attire when attending church, seems to be of no importance or does not matter to some of today's

Christian churches. We are taught that the Lord only sees the heart and not the outward appearance. However, we forget that others can be affected by the types of clothes we wear to church, especially if we wear sexy and provocative clothing.

Another problem that the church of Ephesus was facing was that some of the women wore inappropriate and indecent attire to the worship services, which caused distraction and caused men to lust. Today, we also confront the same issues. Every year, especially in the summer, we are bombarded by new trends that are very sensual and are exhibited mainly by models and celebrities on TV. One time I heard a model say, "Ladies, be careful in following all the trends out there because not all of them are meant to fit your body and your style." I must say that I have to agree with this lady and if I may, I'd like to add that not all trends are decent. During the summer, I noticed that women tend to wear less clothes or more revealing apparel due to either the hot weather or because they want to fit in with the crowd and the latest trends.

What is the apostle Paul saying to us? I believe that He's trying to tell us, (and I'm going to paraphrase him in my own words) "Hey Missy, it's OK to dress cool as long as you look honorable. I do not expect you to wear Biblical robes as your normal apparel. Times have changed and styles have too, but just remember that as you dress up in these modern times, clothe yourself with decency and modesty. Be careful with following the worldly trends that are designed for women to flaunt their sexuality and pride. You can dress trendy but not trashy, feminine but not sensual. Be wise as you choose your clothing when shopping. Christian women should not dress to cause others to lust over them but dress in a way that is pure and that may glorify God."

Propriety

Propriety is the last principle of the three stated by the apostle Paul concerning Christian women's attire (1 Tim. 2:9). The Greek word for propriety is *sophrosyne*.[49] It is defined as "moderation and sensibility." The apostle Paul is indicating that we are to dress not only modestly and with decency, but also with propriety, which means we are to have sensibility and be conscious of what type of clothes we put on wherever we go and to whatever event we attend. There is appropriate clothing for all occasions, and a time and a place for each style. Would you wear a bridesmaid dress to go horseback riding or sports clothes to a wedding?

Solomon tells us that "...there is a season for every activity under the heavens:" (Eccl. 3:1). There is also appropriate attire for every event on our social calendar. If you were invited to an elegant dinner at the White House and were seated next to the President of United States or were to meet the Queen of England, would you show up wearing a t-shirt, jeans and sneakers? I don't think they would let you in. These particular people are very important and we are required to pay honor, respect and reverence not only with our behavior, but also with our apparel. The book of Esther explains how Esther had to follow a strict beauty regimen before presenting herself to the King **(Esth. 2:12-13)**. In those days, it was important for the girl to dress her best with appropriate clothing. If you had to sing for a special church event, would you step to the altar in your exercise clothing or pajamas? I believe that you would wear your very best for Him. God is a holy God and he deserves our respect and reverence; therefore, we must honor him with our hearts, mind, soul, and body.

As Christian women, it is essential to wear clothes in good taste and be aware of what type of clothing is appropriate to wear when attending worship service. As we enter into His court, we must enter with thanksgiving, a reverent attitude, and a respectful wardrobe (Heb. 12:28). Once again, I would like to emphasize that God's Word is not against fashion, nice clothing and accessories; but rather it admonishes us not to dress in an extreme way that will project pride, vanity and provoke lustful desires. So I would gladly like to encourage you to have fun trying on clothes when shopping; but remember to shop with good judgment and discernment. This will lead you to purchase the right clothing that will allow you to practice modesty, decency, and propriety.

Fashion is in the Heart of God

Earthly fashion designers are constantly creating new clothing every year for their spring, summer, fall, and winter collections. God is also a fashion designer. His fashion is never boring or dull. Everything he creates is beautiful and new. It never goes out of style. He created different colors, styles, and materials for all seasons. Fashion designers may get inspired to create clothing by earth tone colors. For His spring and summer collection, every year, He creates white tulips and all kinds of colorful flowers that grow throughout the land. He dresses the hills with stunning green pastures and paints the summer skies blue. The Psalmist expresses the Lord's work of art in chapter 19 verse 1, "The heavens declare the glory of God; the skies proclaim the work of his hands."

We continue to see His beauty throughout his fall collection as he dresses the trees with exquisite shades of autumn colors of green, red, orange, purple, and so forth. For his winter fashion, he clothes the mountains with pure white snow. He filled the earth with a variety of colors and created different kinds of animals and plants, and made a diversity of people. We come in different shapes and colors, and from diverse cultures. No one can top God's infinite design. Solomon declared that, "He has made everything beautiful in its time…" (Eccles: 3:11, ESV). Since fashion is in the heart of God, it is important that we also care for our outer appearance and how we dress.

Why Should We Care About Our Outer Appearance?

Fashion has to do with dressing oneself with various materials, styles and personal appearance. Some women might say, "Well, I do not care much to dress up nicely, because I don't have time for myself. I'm too busy with life." Others may say, "My husband or boyfriend loves me just the way I am, I do not need to fuss with the external look." Still others assert, "God only cares that I concentrate on beautifying my inner-self, because caring for personal appearance is simply pure vanity." As much as we need to prioritize in caring and beautifying our souls, I also believe that we ought to not neglect our personal appearance. Why? The apostle Paul reminds us that our bodies are the temple of the Holy Spirit (1 Cor. 6:19). How are we going to dress it up? As His temple, we must dress it as best as we can. Here's a case of a woman who learned a valuable lesson concerning outer appearance.

One Saturday morning, a lady I knew decided that she was going to go to the streets to give out Bible tracks and be a witness of Christ to the un-churched people in her neighborhood.

She was so excited about wanting to spread the gospel that she neglected to fix her outer appearance. Grooming and dressing her best was not her priority. As soon as she woke up, she put on an old yellow dress that had holes ripped from the sides and added some green striped socks to go with her outfit. She ate a piece of fruit and didn't even bother to wash her face, leaving signs of food stuck on her face; and furthermore, she did not comb her hair. She looked like a mess and just like that she walked out the door. Later on, she shared with me the outcome of her day. She said to me, that as she was spreading the Bible tracks, people were giving her change money. They thought that she was a beggar in the streets. As she hand over a track to a young man. She said to him, "Jesus loves you and wants to save you." He replied back, "What kind of Jesus are you preaching about? It looks like you're the one who needs to be saved."

This lady learned her lesson. She learned that if she wanted people to take her seriously, she had to start taking care of her outer appearance. Some women concentrate too much on beautifying the soul and neglect the body. We have to have a balance. We are advised through Scripture that since we are His Temple, we must care for it both inwardly and outwardly. Also, let us not forget that as Christ's ambassadors we are viewed as His models (2 Cor. 5:20). Therefore, we ought to dress beautifully according to our means, always in a decent and orderly manner, in order to reflect His glory and represent Him well.

Conclusion

God is pleased when we not only worship Him with a heart robed in humbleness, but also when we dress our bodies in a Godly fashion. We must remember that our bodies are the Temple of the Holy Ghost. In what ways or styles are we going to dress it up? It is also imperative to keep in mind, that as we step out of our homes, we must take a minute to check if what we are wearing will glorify Him and not us. It is my prayer that as His true wonder women, we will keep these three principles left to us by the apostle Paul as a basic guide that we can implement within our sense of style and fashion. As Christian women, according to Scripture, we are expected to dress *modestly,* with *decency* and *propriety.* As we apply these Biblical principles, we will glorify the Father. Also, our attire will make a statement that will say to the world: "We are classy, elegant, and poised; well put together godly women dressed in a God's true wonder woman fashion.

Prayer for Discernment

Dear Heavenly Father, I thank You for caring for the smallest details of our lives. You care that our hearts are clothed with your holiness and that our outward appearance will also reflect Your image. As I am bombarded by the influence of worldly fashions and trends, I ask You to please give me wisdom and discernment, in order that I may choose the right clothes and styles that would allow me to dress modestly, with decency, and with propriety, as stated in Your Word. It is my desire that my inward and outward appearance will bring You honor and glory. In Jesus name I pray. Amen!

Chapter Eight

God is tickled by you. "The Lord God is with you...He will take great delight in you, He will quiet you with His love, He will rejoice over you with singing."
(Zeph. 3:17)

Celebrate the True Wonder Woman in You

*M*iriam had much reason to celebrate and commemorate the day of her freedom. She and her family, and her entire Jewish community, had been placed in bondage and in slavery for many years. She had also suffered the pain of watching her baby brother Moses be raised by her enemies. Ever since her childhood, all she knew was a life of misery, poverty, and oppression. When she was a child, she did not know what it was to play with dolls, have birthday parties, or even have a sleepover with friends. As a teenager, she did not have the luxury of having her own bedroom decorated with posters of her favorite pop-stars. When she grew into a woman, she did not have the comforts and amenities that we are used to having at our home. Her enemies had given her a life of imprisonment. Furthermore, she suffered needs, pains and abuse, until one glorious day, the Lord set Miriam, her family, and her community free!

The book of Exodus, speaks about how she and her people suffered greatly at the hands of the Egyptians. God then sent Moses, her long lost brother and chosen one, to lead them out of captivity from a horrible dictator called Pharaoh (Exod. 3:10). The Lord delivered them. He divided the waters of the Red Sea, and they were able to escape (Exod. 14:21-22). When they had crossed over the other side, the all Mighty One caused the waters to flow back in their place destroying the Egyptians who were following them. (Exod. 14:26-28).

As soon as Miriam and the rest made it, they began to sing with happiness, celebrating their deliverance from their enemies and from captivity. They danced and sang a song of victory because they were no longer captives (Exod. 15:1). The Lord had set Miriam and her people free for the following purposes: They were set free so that they could worship God freely without any restrictions (Exod. 9:1). They were also set free so that they could pursue their promised land (Num. 14:8).

The Lord's intentions were for Miriam and her people to live not in misery but to have a life filled with His love, peace, joy, and to experience spiritual growth and abundant blessings. In her new found freedom, God was offering this woman a new life where she would have a chance to grow in Him and discover her potentials and her strengths. The

Lord's desire was for her to have an opportunity to discover and celebrate the wonder woman in her.

It is Satan's goal to oppress us and put us in a state of spiritual bondage. God offers us a life of new opportunities where we can experience true freedom and joy in our spirits. We can obtain it by allowing Christ to rule our hearts. Being in Christ allows us to live freely from the bondage of sin and the enemy's oppression. In Him, we are free to worship God without any holdups and to love wholeheartedly. We are empowered to conquer our promise land, to conquer all our fears and reach our true potentials and dreams. In Christ, we build characteristics of a true wonder woman and are able to find our true identity (1 Pet. 2:9). Before God made the earth, He thought about you and saw what you could become in His hands. He saw the true wonder woman in you and from that moment on, He's been celebrating you. He also wants you to live a life that celebrates who you are in Christ and the things you can accomplish through His mighty power; so therefore, I encourage you to continuously discover and celebrate the true wonder woman in you (Ps. 16:11).

You are Celebrated by God

If the thought ever crossed your mind that maybe you're not special or that you're ordinary, someone above surely thinks the opposite. In God's eyes you are extraordinary. You are His most ultimate and precious creation, and to Him, your life is valued more than anything in this world. If only you could understand how much you are worth and loved by your Heavenly Father.

There are so many reasons why you and I are celebrated by our Creator. I will mention a few. He celebrates us because *we are wonderfully made*. Did you know that you were created uniquely? There is no one in this world that has your same or exact DNA and fingerprints, not even your twin, if you have one. God made you exclusive, exquisite and incomparable. Our Heavenly Father celebrates our distinctive beauty, personalities, talents, gifts, qualities and potentials. To Him, we are exceptional regardless of our skin color, shape, weight, age, race, circumstances, status, background, and genes. There's no other Creator on earth that could create such a marvelous creation as you and I. The Psalmist expresses how God's hand beautifully made us in the secret place of our mother's womb. You and I are truly His work of art. He asserts, "For you created my inmost being; you knit me together in my mother's womb. I praise you because I am fearfully and wonderfully made; your works are wonderful, I know that full well. My frame was not hidden from you when I was made in the secret place..." (139:13-15).

God also celebrates *our redemption*. Although we were once destined to die in eternal condemnation, through Jesus' blood at Calvary we are redeemed (1 Pet. 1:18-19). We ought not to fear in shame when approaching our Heavenly Father for help and support. When we repent and turn away from our sins, Christ's blood cleanses us from all of our transgressions and God will no longer remember our past sins (Micah 7:19). Therefore, we can come boldly to Him, knowing that we have been forgiven. It is the Lord's desire that as His true wonder women we will live out our lives, in spite of our trials, freely from guilt and shame, always walking as His redeemed children.

God celebrates *our friendship.* Some people tend to look at God as a master of the universe who sits on His throne only to give orders and dictate our lives, but the Lord is more relational than we can imagine. He celebrates us not as acquaintances and not as slaves or servants, but rather as His personal friends. In the book of John, Jesus calls us friends (15:15). When we care to deeply connect with Him and follow Him, He treats us as His friends. Abraham who was an ordinary man had a very close relationship with the Lord. He was called a friend of God because He believed in His Word and kept His covenant (Jm. 2:23). True friends believe, trust and confide with one another. God is pleased with us when we believe in Him and seek His face. He gets very excited when you talk and share all of your most intimate secrets with Him. He also wishes to take part of every detail of your life, in order to help and guide you to reach your God-given destiny. It is His desire that you may obtain victories and success in your journey. As you open your heart to Him, He too will reveal His divine plans for your life. The Psalmist knew how to get to God's heart by pursuing a deep relationship with Him and in return, the Lord confided His promises to him (Ps. 25:14).

God also celebrates and honors *our faith.* Abraham was seventy five years old when the Lord called him out of his family's home (Gen. 12:4). He did not have any children and longed for a child. The Lord made a promise to grant him a son in His time (Gen. 12:7). It took approximately twenty-five years before Abraham could see God's promises come to life, but his faith in God did not waver; as he waited in Him, he continued to believe. He was one hundred years old when his wife (who was ninety at the time) gave birth to his son,

Isaac (Gen. 21:5). Miracles can happen in our lives when we believe and wait upon Him. In His time, He will reward and celebrate our ever strong faith.

In the same manner that the Lord rewards our faith, He also celebrates *our courage when we are willing to suffer for the cause of Christ.* Our Lord Jesus suffered hurts, sorrows and the pain of death at the cross for us. As His daughters, we too will not be exempt from suffering some pain and injustice in this world; especially when we are called to speak the good news of the gospel and might suffer rejection because of it. As a result of our courage, we become co-heirs with Christ. The apostle Paul tells us that we are truly co-heirs with Jesus, if we are not afraid to share in his sufferings (Rom. 8:17). As we endure some earthly sufferings, we are encouraged to keep and maintain a kind heart.

God rejoices and celebrates a woman with *a kind heart.* King Solomon asserts that we earn the Lord's respect when we act in kindness, "A kindhearted woman gains respect" (Prov. 11:16). Did you know that we can make God smile and sing? The honorable and kind things that we do produce joy in His heart. Did you also know that He has a song with your name on it? As you obey His commands and love Him, His Word tells us that He is so delighted with you that He sings about you and over you (Zeph. 3:17). *As His loving child, He is simply tickled by you.* Have you ever heard Him sing? You can, if you open your heart to hear His voice. His love will gently sooth your soul. In the quiet hours of the night, as you rest your mind from the cares of the day and open up your heart; you'll hear him sing you a lullaby as His Word resonates through your spirit, thus bringing a sweet melody of calmness into your weary soul.

Likewise, our whole being can rest peacefully in the Lord, as we trust Him with our future. God also celebrates *our future* because He knows it very well. In the book of Jeremiah, chapter 29:11, we are told to chill out, keep it together, sit back, and wait for it. What exactly are you saying, Pastor Evie? I mean to wait patiently for that better thing to happen in your life. As I humbly interpret this verse in my own words, I'm imagining that He is trying to say, "Hey pretty woman, relax! Your life is in my hand. I have it all under control. Be aware though that all the good, the bad, and the ugly is allowed in your life in order to shape you and your future. So don't panic, just trust me." The Lord asserts, "For I know the plans I have for you, declares the Lord, plans to prosper you and not to harm you, plans to give you hope and a future" (Jer. 29:11). If the enemy has told you that your future does not look too bright due to either a failure in your relationship, an enduring sickness, or a bad career; whatever hardships you may be going through, in the midst of it all, God is celebrating your future with great optimism. As humans, we only see pieces of the puzzles of our lives; however, the Lord sees the whole picture of the puzzle completed. When things do not go as we expect them to, we must trust in Him. He is rearranging the pieces, placing them all together so they can fit into his divine plan for you. The apostle Paul encourages us that all will work out in the end for those who love the Lord (Rom. 8:28).

I could go on and on as to why God celebrates you, but the most important reason that you are celebrated by Him, is simply because *He loves you, deeply*. No one loves you more in this world than your Heavenly Father. You are His main focus and the apple of His eye. His eyes will follow you wherever you go to bless you and to protect you from all harm. The Psalmist declared his position within the Lord's heart. He says, "Keep me as the apple of your eye; hide me in the shadow of your wings." (Ps. 17:8). If ever you feel unloved, think about God's infinite love over you. He will never quit loving you. His love will cover you, heal you and provide for you.

Not only does God love you, but He will also put a special someone in your life to love you through Him. As His special true wonder women, the Lord will make sure that somebody, whether you are aware of it or not, will celebrate you and your accomplishments. It could be your family, husband, children, boyfriend, friends, coworkers, neighbors, or admirers. I must say that we do not need to depend on people's applause in order to know that we are special to God. Eventually, we will be celebrated not only in heaven but also here on earth by those around us. Through Him, our lives shine and His goodness in us can affect others in a positive way.

You are Celebrated by Those Around You

When I was a child, I remember listening to a song played in the radio called "You don't have to be a star (to be in my show)" sung by Marilyn McCoo and Billy Davis, Jr.[50] Whenever I heard it; it made me feel important. That song had so much meaning. I have realized that we do not have to have our names written down in a big star on the Hollywood Walk of Fame or be a celebrity in order to shine or touch someone else's life. All we have to do is be ourselves.

A woman has the ability to affect and influence her surroundings. With her special charms, she can positively calm the moods of others. One afternoon, I was sitting down at a McDonalds having coffee with my husband and oldest daughter. We were having a serene moment enjoying our drink, until two tall grown men walked in and sat behind us. Our quiet time soon began to dissipate when these men turned to one another and started to yell loudly with angry voices. They were arguing about some silly thing. Frankly, I got scared thinking they were going to kill each other. All of a sudden this woman walked in, and directing herself toward the men, gave them a big smile and greeting. The horrific yelling behind me turned to joyful laughter. I looked at my daughter and said, "Now that's what you call *Women Power*, baby! That woman with her smile and gentle voice had the power to quiet those two giants. She was truly a superstar doing her magic in her own show.

What is it that attracts people to admire and mimic superstars? They sparkle for their beauty, appearance, gifts and talents. You don't have to be a celebrity in order to be famous and be able to impact people. You are a superstar in the sight of your Heavenly Father, family, friends, community and peers at work or school. Through God's grace in us, we can make a difference. Every woman has her own abilities and special talents that she can utilize to bless others. Whenever you feel less of yourself or that you are not special enough, pay attention to the compliments that are given to you by those around you. As a mom, whenever I cook something delicious for my family, after they finish eating, my daughters quickly tell me, "Mom, that dish was the bomb! You're the best cook in town!" It makes me feel good inside and it also makes me realize that as they complement me, I'm celebrated by my family for my cooking skills.

When someone asks you for advice, copies your style of clothing, longs for your friendship, or acknowledges you or your work, it means that you as a person have something special to offer and have impacted their lives in some big or small way. When they speak about you, good or bad, do not be troubled. Take it as a compliment. You might not be a star making headlines on the news, but you sure are in their world, because you are important enough to be talked about.

Allow me to reiterate: Never forget that you are very special to God and that He has given you many good qualities, whether you have discovered them or have yet to do so. He will always send you a message through someone, letting you know that your life and accomplishments are being celebrated by Him, those around you, or others that you might not even be aware of, that have been touched by your life in some ways.

When the prophet Elijah was hiding in his cave, he felt alone and depressed. After they had killed the prophets of God, he thought that he was the only one standing, but the Lord reassured him that there were still seven thousand people who had not bowed down to Baal (1 King 19:14, 18). Somehow, Elijah's life and ministry had influenced many people positively and he did not even know about it until the Lord made him aware of it. A woman filled with Christ lives a life that touches and influences others for the good, and in return she is celebrated by those she has impacted. Solomon asserts how the life of a true wonder woman ought to be celebrated. He says, "…a woman who fears the Lord is to be praised. Honor her for all that her hands have done, and let her works bring her praise at the city gate." (Prov. 31:30-31).

Celebrate With Thankfulness

How can we celebrate the true wonder woman in us? We can do so when we recognize who we are in Christ, all that we have attained through Him, and all that we will continue to achieve through His strength and power. Celebrate with thankfulness God's gifts of salvation, family and friends. There is an old Hymn song that has always ministered to me. The first line is "Count your many blessings, name them one by one."[51] When we focus primarily on the things that we long for but have yet to obtain, we become frustrated; however, if we reflect and count every blessing that the Lord has bestowed upon us, this will produce joy in our hearts and we will find plenty of reasons to celebrate. Celebrate all that the Lord has done for you (Ps. 136:1- 4).

Conclusion

It is God's desire that as He rejoices over your life, your accomplishments, your worship unto Him, and your future, that you may not walk entangled by life's worries, fears and hardships. Rather, He wishes that you may appreciate and recognize all those things that come from Him that can empower you to discover and celebrate the true wonder woman in you. It is my prayer that through this book, you may be inspired to pursue a closer relationship with the Lord.

As you seek His presence and His Word, His Holy Spirit will guide you to find and release your God-given powers. If you are confronting physical or emotional distress from the effects of sexual abuse, hormonal imbalance, or restlessness from the Do it All Syndrome, it is also my prayer that your strength may be multiplied. May He also grant you His wisdom and discernment to pursue and build a Christ-like attitude toward how to dress your inward as well as your outward attire. Be assured that as a woman of God, you are no longer subjected to the bondage of sin and Satan, but that through Christ you have been redeemed and are now living in His freedom. King Solomon describes how your Creator and Heavenly Father feels about you. In His eyes, you are *His True Wonder Woman*. He says, "Many women do noble things, but **you surpass them all** [bold letters added for emphasis]" (Prov. 31: 29). If you are in need of strength to continue on in your spiritual journey, please join me in this prayer.

Prayer for Strength in Your Journey

Dear Heavenly Father, thank You for celebrating me as Your redeemed daughter. It is my desire to build a great relationship with You. I ask You to give me strength to carry on and power to overcome all of my obstacles. Through You, I know that I can conquer it all. Once again, I pray for strength, power, courage, faith, hope, love and endurance as I continue on this journey to discover the true wonder woman in me. Thank You my Heavenly Father. In Jesus name I pray. Amen!

Prayer for Salvation

If you have not yet accepted Christ as your personal Lord and Savior and would like to receive Him in your heart, can you make this prayer with me? After you do, I recommend that you continuously seek the Lord in prayer, meditate in His Word, and also, look for a church that would minister to you and where you can congregate with God's saints. Please repeat the Sinner's Prayer with me:

Heavenly Father, I come to you broken and hurt. I humble myself, recognizing that I am a sinner and am in need of you. Please come into my heart. I accept you as my Lord and Savior and renounce my heart to the world and to sin. Cleanse me with the blood of Jesus and make me new. Please set me free from all of Satan's bondages and allow me to experience Christ' freedom in the spirit. Fill me with your Holy Spirit and with your joy and peace. Renew my mind and as I surrender my life to you, please write my name in the book of life, that I may live with you someday in heaven to enjoy a never ending celebration of eternal life. I ask all this in Jesus name. Amen.

If this book or any part of it has blessed your life, and you would like to share a testimony or have a prayer request, I would like to hear from you. I'm also available for speaking engagements. You can reach me at **eviewwb@gmail.com** and also through Facebook (Evie Morales). God bless you.

NOTES

Chapter 1

1 W. Gesenius and S.P. Tregelles, *'Gesenius' Hebrew and Chaldee lexicon to the Old Testament Scriptures* (Bellingham, WA, 2003): 264.

2 K.A. Mathews, *The New American Commentary: Genesis 1-11:26* (Broadman & Holman Publishers: Nashville, 1996): Vol. 1A, 254.

3 Ibid. Vol. 1A, 239.

4 J. Strong, *Enhanced Strong's Lexicon* (Bellingham, WA, 2001).

5 W.D. Reyburn and E.M. Fry, *A Handbook on Genesis* (United Bible Societies: New York, 1998): 93.

6 J. Swanson, *Dictionary of Biblical Languages with Semantic Domains: Hebrew Old Testament,* Electronic ed. (Logos Research Systems, Inc. 2001).

7 Mathew Henry, *Matthew Henry's Commentary on the Whole Bible: Complete and Unabridged in One Volume* (Peabody: Hendrickson, 1994): 14.

8 Ibid.

9 Ibid. 10.

10 Ibid. 14.

11 Mary Elizabeth Baxter, *Eve-Genesis 2:18*, Blue Letter Bible. http://www.blueletterbible.org/commentaries/baxter_mary/ (accessed Aug.18, 2015).

12 Steven James, *Becoming Real: Christ's call to Authentic Living* (Howard Publishing co: United States, 2005):140.

13 Ibid.

14 Ibid.

Chapter 2

15 Herbert Lockyer, *Mary Magdalene: The Woman Who Had Seven Devils* (Zondervan, 1988):1 Mary Magdalene, The Woman who had the seven demons, article of Bible gateway 1988 Zondervan http://www.biblegateway.com/resources/all-women-bible/Mary-Magdalene (Accessed June 15)

Chapter 3

16 Bobby Houston, *I'll Have what She's Having* (Maximized Leadership Press: Australia, 1998):5.

17 Ibid. 710.

18 D. Seal, "Ephesus", In (J. D. Barry & L. Wentz, Eds.) *The Lexham Bible Dictionary* (Lexham Press: Bellingham, WA, 2012).

19 C. Church, "Fertility Cult." In (C. Brand, C. Draper, A. England, S. Bond, E.R. Clendenen, & T.C Butler, Eds.) *Holman Illustrated Bible Dictionary* (Holman Bible Publishers: Nashville, TN, 2003): 566.

20 Ibid. 679.

21 J.P Louw, and E.A. Nida, *Greek-English Lexicon of the New Testament: based on semantic domains* (United Bible Societies: New York, 1996): electronic ed. of the 2nd edition, Vol.1, 679.

22 J. Strong, *Enhanced Strong's Lexicon* (Woodside Bible Fellowship, 1995).

23 Alex Ness, *The Holy Spirit-Volume Two* (Christian Centre Publication: Ontario, Canada, 1980): 8.

24 Ibid. 9.

25 Ibid. 57.

26 H.D.M. Spence-Jones, (Ed.). "Ephesians" (Funk & Wagnalls Company: London; New York:1909): 259.

27 J. Swanson, *Dictionary of Biblical Languages with Semantic Domains: Greek New Testament,* electronic ed. (Logos Research Systems, Inc. 1997).

28 G. Kittel, G.W. Bromiley, and G. Friedrich, (Eds.) *Theological dictionary of the New Testament* (Eerdmans: Grand Rapids, MI, 1964): Vol. 5, p. 312 (electronic ed.).

29 Ibid.

Chapter 4

30 J. Strong, *Enhanced Strong's Lexicon* (Woodside Bible Fellowship: 1995).

31 Ibid.

32 Malcolm Smith, *Spiritual Burnout: When doing all you can isn't enough* (Honor Books: Tulsa, Ok, 1988): 11.

33 Roger, Heuser, class notes taken in 2005.

Chapter 5

34 Safehorizon, *"Rape & Sexual Assault":*1 http://www.safehorizon.org/page/rape—sexual-assault-54.html?gclid=CKqs_vj1I8QCFRCqaQodlZgAdQ (accessed March 17, 2015).

35 World Health Organization, *"Violence against Women: Intimate partner and Sexual Violence against women"* (Fact sheet N°239, November 2014):2 http://www.who.int/mediacentre/factsheets/fs239/en/ (accessed April 18, 2015).

36 Black MC, Basile KC, Breiding MJ, Smith SG, Walters ML, Merrick MT, Chen J, Stevens MR. *The National Intimate Partner and Sexual Violence Survey (NISVS): 2010 Summary Report.* Atlanta, GA: National Center

for Injury Prevention and Control, Centers for Disease Control and Prevention; 2011. http://www.cdc.gov/ViolencePrevention/pdf/sv-datasheet-a.pdf (accessed, March 12, 2016).

37 Tracy C. Hohnson, MD, FACOG, "Your Guide to Sexual Transmitted Diseases, WebMD (September 8, 2014):1 http://wwwwebmd.com/sexual-health-stds#1 (accessed, March 12, 2016

Chapter 6

38 Melissa Conrad Stoppler, MD, William C. Shiel Jr, MD, "Premenstrual Syndrome (Cont.)? Medicine Net.com (August 19,2014):4 http://www.medicine net.com/premenstrual syndrome/page4.htm (accessed, September 5, 2014).

39 Shannon K. Laughlin-Tommaso, MD, The Mayo Clinic Staff "Perimenopause," Mayo Clinic (April 20, 2013):1 http://www.mayoclinic.org/about-this-site/meet-our-medical-editors (accessed, September 6, 2015).

40 Elizabeth Lee Vliet, M.D., *It's My Ovaries Stupid*, (Her Place Press: Tucson, AZ, 2007): 88.

Chapter 7

41 Spence-Jones, H. D. M (Ed.). *Genesis* (Funk & Wagnalls Company: London, New York, 1909): 52.

42 J.P. Lange, P. Schaff, T. Lewis & A. Gosman, *A Commentary on the Holy Scriptures: Genesis* (Bellingham, WA: 2008): 240.

43 Bentley, M. *Opening up Zephaniah* (Leominster Day One Publications: 2008):30.

44 C.F. Pfeiffer, *The Wycliffe Bible Commentary: Old Testament (Ex 20:22)* (Moody Press: Chicago, 1962).

45 Ibid. 33.

46 J. Strong, *Enhanced Strong's Lexicon* (Woodside Bible Fellowship, 1995).

47 R. C. H. Lenski, *The interpretation of St. Paul's Epistles to the Colossians, to the Thessalonians, to Timothy, to Titus and to Philemon*, (Lutheran Book Concern: Columbus, OH, 1937): 560.

48 Ibid.

49 Ibid.

Chapter 8

50 Marilyn McCoo and Billy Davis Jr., "You Don't Have to Be a Star (To Be In My Show)" I hope we get to love in time (LP) ABC Record, 1976.

51 Johnson Oatman Jr. and Edwin O. Excell, "Count your blessings," *Songs for Young People* (Chicago, Illinois: 1897) <u>cyberhymnal.org/htm/c/o/countyou.htm</u> (accessed, January 11, 2016).

About the Author

Rev. Evelyn Morales is an ordained minister of the Assemblies of God. She has served in ministry for over 30 years as a contemporary Christian singer, associate pastor, Bible school teacher and a conference speaker. In 2006, she obtained a Master's degree in theological studies at Vanguard University. She and her husband, Dr. Maynor Morales, were senior pastors at New Dawn Worship Center in Fremont, California for over 15 years, and are currently opening a new Church in Fort Worth, Texas. They are parents of two beautiful daughters. Evelyn has had the privilege of traveling throughout the United States, Central America, Europe, Asia, Australia and many other parts of the world, ministering the Word of God. One of her greatest passions is to minister to the needs of broken women who need to hear that there is a savior called Jesus who can save, heal, and restore their lives. For more information about how you can invite Pastor Evelyn (she is better known as Evie) to speak to your women's group or conference, you may contact her via email (eviewwb@gmail.com), Facebook: Evie Morales or you may write to her at P.O. Box 136761 Lake Worth, TX 76136.

CPSIA information can be obtained
at www.ICGtesting.com
Printed in the USA
FSOW03n1905190416
19440FS